THE GOSPEL

OF

THE GRACE OF GOD

THE GOSPEL
OF
THE GRACE OF GOD

THOMAS SPURGEON

SOLID GROUND CHRISTIAN BOOKS
BIRMINGHAM, ALABAMA USA

Solid Ground Christian Books
PO Box 660132
Vestavia Hills AL 35266
205-443-0311
mike.sgcb@gmail.com
www.solid-ground-books.com

THE GOSPEL OF THE GRACE OF GOD
Sermons Delivered During His Father's Illness
Thomas Spurgeon (1856-1917)
Preface by C.H. Spurgeon

First published in 1884 by Passmore & Alabaster in London

First Solid Ground edition published in May 2013

Cover design by Borgo Design
Contact them at borgogirl@bellsouth.net

ISBN- 978-159925-286-5

THE
GOSPEL OF THE GRACE OF GOD.

BEING SERMONS DELIVERED AT THE

METROPOLITAN TABERNACLE,

BY

THOMAS SPURGEON,

DURING HIS FATHER'S ILLNESS.

WITH A PREFACE BY C. H. SPURGEON.

London:
PASSMORE AND ALABASTER, PATERNOSTER BUILDINGS.

1884.

CONTENTS.

	PAGE.
"IF THOU CANST!"	11
FINDING THE SAVIOUR	27
LYDIA AND THE JAILOR	41
COMING TO JESUS	57
A WHITE STONE	73
HEARING AND HEARKENING	87
A FAIR WIND	103

THOMAS SPURGEON.

AUCKLAND TABERNACLE—PASTOR, THOMAS SPURGEON.

PREFACE.

Dear Reader,

These Sermons have given great delight to the friends at the Metropolitan Tabernacle. Their pastor was laid low by that painful infirmity which so often attacks him, and his son occupied the pulpit, to his father's great comfort. When the father expressed in public his hearty thanks to Almighty God that his lack of service had been so well supplied by his own son, there was a general assent to the thanksgiving. The verdict of the church was unanimous: the people of God had been fed, and there were not lacking testimonies that sinners had been converted. Old believers, who know the taste of heavenly food, declared that they had been well fed; while the younger folk, with natural enthusiasm, expressed their delight at what they had heard. The praise rendered unto the Lord by many was an offering of sweet savour. So precious a result made it good to have been afflicted, good to have received help from the Lord out of one's own house, and, best of all, to have kindled thousands of hearts with the fire of holy praise and sympathetic gratitude.

These Sermons were taken down by the reporter, and, when printed, a modest request was made, that as soon as father could sit up to do a little work, he would kindly write a brief preface for his son. The preface is needless, but how could the request be refused? What, then, does a preface mean in this case? Well, it means—*God bless these discourses in the reading, as he has blessed them in the hearing*—so far it is a prayer most earnestly presented. May the Lord answer it. It means also an introduction of a new comer by an affectionate word from one who has been longer upon the field. Friends, here stands among you another witness for Christ, upon whom the Spirit of God is resting. He has been up and down in the colonies for years, but on this occasion he speaks from London. We present to you certain of the messages which he has delivered for his Master—messages full of present power, and bright with prophecies of future usefulness if life be spared. Pray for our son, that his ministry, so happily commenced, may equal anything that has preceded it, so that, when the present generation shall have passed away, the younger stock may bear to the front the old, old banner of free-grace and dying love.

In truth, this preface is superfluous. The pastor of the baptized Church of Christ in Auckland, New Zealand, is quite able to speak for himself. Those who shall read these discourses will be of our mind upon that matter. From "Brighter Britain" our son has come to visit us in our best weather; but when the first frosts and fogs of winter surround our misty isle he must be gone, like the swallows, to a sunnier clime. He will leave us this little volume as a *souvenir*, and he will send us papers for *The Sword and the Trowel* as forget-me-nots; meantime, we will entreat the Lord God of his fathers to be with him, and to make him on the other side of the world a wise Master-builder, a workman that needeth not to be ashamed, rightly dividing the word of truth.

Precious things will sell themselves; all that is required of us is just to say,—here are pearls, examine them and estimate them after the manner of merchants who care for nothing but intrinsic worth.

Yours truly,

C. H. SPURGEON.

WESTWOOD,
  September, 1884.

"IF THOU CANST!"

"If thou canst believe, all things are possible to him that believeth."
—*Mark* ix. 23.

THE revised version reads thus:— "And Jesus said unto him, If thou canst! All things are possible to him that believeth." The word "believe" is omitted, and the structure of the sentence entirely altered.

Without presuming to say which is the correct translation, I intend to give you yet another. We will combine the two and read it thus:—"If thou canst! Believe! All things are possible to him that believeth."

Coming at once to the text, we find in it first an *exclamation*—"If thou canst!" Secondly, an *exhortation*—"Believe;" and thirdly, an *explanation*. "All things are possible to him that believeth."

I. Let us consider CHRIST'S EXCLAMATION — "If thou canst!"

A great deal depends upon tone of voice; and though I cannot be certain about the expression and the tone which Jesus used, I am inclined to think that he was so astonished at the unbelief of this poor man whose boy was possessed with a dumb spirit that he took the unbelieving words, "If thou canst," and threw them back in his face, not hard enough to hurt him, not unkindly and ungenerously—that they might appear to him as they had seemed to Christ, faithless and full of doubt. Jesus, perhaps, drew himself back, and looking the sorrowing father reprovingly in the face, said to him ere yet his unbelieving murmurs had died away, "If thou canst! If thou canst!" It was an expression, therefore, of genuine surprise, as if Christ had said, "Do you not know me? Am I a stranger altogether to you, that you are wondering whether I am able to do this little matter for you? Do you fancy that I am as one of these disciples to whom you have applied in vain? Do you not recognise that I am not mere man, but that my arm is omnipotent, and that help has been laid upon one that is mighty to save? Do you not know that this world on which you walk was made by me, and that I have swung it in mid-air, sustaining it by the word of my power? Are you not aware that these hands of mine, as easily as the potter forms the clay upon the wheel, moulded all the worlds and then sent them bowling along their shining tracks? Have you not discovered that without me was not anything made that was made, that I am both Maker and Upholder of all things, and that by me all things consist? O man, you have made a great mistake. You think that you have come to some poor, weak, puny man like my disciples, who could not cast him out; but in very deed you have come to one who, though a man, is just as much a God, to whom this matter is as mere child's-play. 'If thou canst! If thou canst!'" And is it not as if he said to him, "Why, man, have you not heard of my wonderful works to the children of men? If you do not believe in me now that you see and hear me, believe

me for my very works' sake. Have you never heard how
the man that was so stricken with the palsy that he quivered
like an aspen leaf was nerved and invigorated by one word
of mine? Has the voice of rumour never carried the glad
tidings to you that once in the synagogue a withered arm
hung down beside a poor man's side, and that I bade him
stretch it out, and gave him power to do so, and it was
restored whole as the other? Have you not heard about
blind men on whose sightless eyeballs the light of day has
been made to shine because I have said 'Ephphatha,' be
opened? Know you not that lepers have been cleansed at
a word from me—that women have received their dead
children back to life again, and that Lazarus' sepulchre gave
up its dead before my wonder-working voice? Are these
things—matters of history as they are—unknown to you?
They must be, or you surely would not say to me, 'If thou
canst'; and so I say to thee again, 'If thou canst!' Why,
of course I can. I can multiply loaves and fishes to feed
the thousands. I can bid the leper wash and be clean. I
can make the born-blind man return seeing. The very
charnel-houses are subject to my sceptre and my sway, and
I make death's victims walk forth into newness of life. Why,
faithless man, of course I can. It is but what I am doing
every day of my life, healing and blessing, and 'doing good.'
I cast out a legion of devils a while ago: the dumb demon
in thy boy shall flee before my voice."

Now, bringing the subject home to ourselves, I want you
to hear the voice of Christ saying to such of you as are
unbelieving—to such of you as fancy that your case is
altogether beyond his power, "If thou canst! If thou
canst!" My brother, he is God and not man, else he could
not save you. He is God and not angel, for I cannot

believe that the strongest seraph could do a hand's turn to my salvation. I would not trust the whole of the armies of God to redeem my immortal soul. Their fiery footsteps might be quenched; their ardent vigour might at last grow cold; and the very wings with which they cleave the sky might moult their feathers, and their strong pinions lose their wonted power. But my Saviour is "the same yesterday, and to-day, and for ever"—a Redeemer who is "mighty to save." Besides, I know this of Jesus—that he has been anointed to the special work. Upon his head the holy oil has flowed, trickling down, thank God, to the very skirts of his priestly garments. I know that God himself has laid his hands upon his dear Son's head, and bidden him go upon the errand of his mercy; and this assures me that Jesus is able to save, for he is none other than the Christ, the Anointed of the living God. O great High Priest, for ever, after Melchisedec's order, thou shalt never faint or fail; and being thus eternal, immortal and invisible, thou art gloriously and "abundantly able to save," even to the uttermost, all that come unto God by thee!

If I wanted any further proof of Christ's power to save me, he could refer me, as I have supposed he pointed this man, to the cases which he had already healed. I do not know any greater encouragement for those who find it difficult to believe that Christ is able to save *them*, than the very evident fact that he has saved so many before them. Think of Manasseh, perhaps one of the vilest sinners, who filled Jerusalem with innocent blood from one end to the other, who caused his sons and daughters to pass through the fire, and set up a graven image of the grove in the temple of the living God. And yet even he is found with broken heart and tearful eyes turning to the Lord God of his fathers, and God receives and pardons him, and, for the sake of the blood that was yet to be spilt, Manasseh became a forgiven sinner. Remember the sinful woman who came to weep at Jesus' feet. Who shall recite the catalogue of her crimes? And yet he said to her, turning from the proud Pharisees who thought that they had no need of repentance, "Woman, thy sins *which are many* are all forgiven thee." Saul of Tarsus was about the best judge of himself, and he declares that he was the very chief of sinners. Oh, well then, there is hope for me and hope for everybody else, for where Paul could get through I can find entrance, and where the chiefest has gone the rest can follow. Is it not so? Yes; I verily believe that he who sits on the door-step of hell, and scarcely has a dog to lick his sores, through faith in the strong arm of a mighty Saviour, and in the blood of the everlasting covenant, may rest with Lazarus in Abraham's bosom, or better still, within the sheltering arms of Jesus. Oh, if thou art here to-night, a foul and filthy sinner, do not mind that I call you so. Call yourself so; and then come away to Jesus, for he is *abundantly able to save.* The devil-dragged sinners of this poor sin-cursed world shall yet be led in chains of everlasting love and light, behind the glowing chariot wheels of our Emmanuel, and sing more sweet, more loud, than they whose sins were less, the song of Moses and the Lamb, praising for ever and for evermore the grace that picked them from the dunghill and set them amongst princes. God through Jesus is the great Physician. Though he has a hospital, as I believe, for every case, there is none for incurables. "How so?" says some one, "I thought that his hospital was specially for incurables." So it is in one sense, for we are incurable indeed till he takes us in hand;

but I mean that as soon as we go to him we cease to be incurables. He never said of any patient, "I can do no more for him, his case is hopeless, his complaint baffles me, and I must give him up!" Not he, indeed! Never has he suffered defeat; and let the case be what it may—however malignant the fever, however long standing the palsy, however hideous the leprosy, however fierce the legion—he can heal, and cleanse, and restore, and deliver. Glory, eternal glory, to his ever blessed name! It has been said, and I think truly, of the Duke of Marlborough, the victor of Ramilies and Oudenarde, and Malplaquet, that he never set siege to a town without taking it, never pursued his enemies without overtaking them, and never engaged in conflict without coming out with conquest. However that may be of him in so horrible a work, this I know of King Jesus—that he has never drawn his sword in vain, never pulled his bow for naught, never put out his healing hand for nothing. Blessed Victor, glorious Conqueror, sweet Champion, we may well bring our sick ones, as ourselves, and lay them at thy feet, for they are safe and happy there! "Lord, to whom shall we go but unto thee?" When the boy in the harvest-field was striken by the sun, his father said, "Carry him to his mother." Where could they carry him better? "Carry him to his mother." And when the sick sinner comes complaining of soul suffering, we may "Carry him to his Saviour"; for as one whom his mother comforteth, so will the Lord console the sin-sick soul.

I think that the Lord Jesus spoke to this man in a tone of tender pity, as if with tears in his eyes he said to him, "Oh, poor man, is it this that has been troubling you? Have you been dreaming that I am not able to help your boy? Well, I shall soon show you that I can. But I am

so sorry for you that this should have worried and wearied
you. Once another came to me and said, 'Lord, if thou
wilt thou canst make me clean,' and now you say, 'Lord, I
believe that thou art willing, but I am not sure whether
thou art able.'" I wonder if the Lord Jesus himself knows
which is the more absurd form of unbelief—to doubt his
ability or to question his willingness to save.

> "He is able, he is willing;
> Doubt no more!"

And in this exclamation of the Lord Jesus I fancy that
there was a tone of kind assurance. His face beamed with
pleasure at the anticipation of seeing the man's face light
up presently, so he said to him, "If thou canst! If thou
canst! I will show you directly that I can, quite readily
and easily." Let me illustrate this point. Suppose that
out in yonder street there stands a lady with a kind
expression on her face, and what perhaps is the best
accompaniment to a loving face, a very well lined purse in
her pocket. She draws forth this purse and gives a poor
man a shilling; and a little crossing-sweeper, who stands
by, thinks to himself, "Dear me, I am out of that, I wish I
had got a shilling, or even a sixpence! Why should not I
go and ask the lady? She looks very kind." So off he
goes, and touching an apology for a cap, says, "Kind lady,
could you give me a penny? Could you give me a
penny?" Then she looks at him and replies, "Could I
give you a penny!" Remember she has her purse full of
glittering sovereigns, half-crowns and shillings, perhaps a
threepenny-piece in between them, but it is almost hidden.
"Could I give you a penny!" she repeats, and then hands
him a shilling straight away. Of course she *could* give him

a penny, her only difficulty being that she hadn't so small a coin; and she could as easily have given him a sovereign as a shilling, for the matter of that. So I go to Jesus and say, "Lord couldst thou save me?" and he says, "Could I save you!" Then, with a great salvation, he stretches out his hand to pull me from the miry clay, and, not content with that, he sets my feet upon a rock, and puts a new song in my mouth. I ask for copper and he gives me gold, for water and he gives me milk. To use another illustration. Here is a poor little boy struggling with a great load almost as big as himself. He has to climb a high hill; but standing at the bottom of it he is wondering however he shall toil to the top. He does try, but it seems almost too much for him, he is so small and weak. Presently a great strong fellow comes along with his coat off. Why he is in his shirt-sleeves I do not know, but he looks as if he wants something to do; so the little fellow goes to him, and says pleadingly, "Could you give me a lift? Could you give me a lift?" Then the great strong man looks down at the small boy, and answers as if amused, "Could I give you a lift! Do you mean yourself, or the parcel, or both?" And down he stoops, and takes up the boy, and the bundle too, and they are away up at the top of the hill before either of them knows the difficulty at all. I, as a sinner, have a burden upon my back, so heavy, that if I do not lose it, or get some one to carry it for me, it will crush me lower every day, and drive me at last to the nethermost hell; and Jesus comes along—"Jesus of Nazareth passeth by," and I cry to him, saying, "Lord, if thou canst do anything, have compassion on me and help me!" "If thou canst!" says he; then lovingly lifts my sin away, and bears the dreadful load. On the hill of Calvary thou, O

"*If thou canst!*"

Christ, hast poured out thy life-blood for my sin! Jesus, I cannot doubt thy power to save, for thou hast assured me that thou art as able as thou art willing. Do you notice how the Lord takes unbelieving prayers and transforms them into assurances to stimulate and increase feeble faith? As he treated this poor suppliant so does he in mercy deal with us. For instance, I say to him, "Lord, is it possible, can it be, that such a sinner as I, on whose black list well nigh every imaginable sin is chronicled, should be washed whiter than snow?" Then listening for the answer from the mercy-seat, I hear the assuring echo, "*Whiter than snow.*" "But, Lord, I am one of those who have sinned against light and knowledge. A mother's tears have bedewed my head as I knelt at her knee. A father's counsels, a pastor's pleadings, and many a heaven-sent message have remained unheeded. My sin is aggravated and inexcusable. Can it be that there is mercy for the vilest?" And, listening once again, the ear of faith catches the sweet voice that sounds aloud from Calvary, "*Mercy for the vilest.*" "Ah, Lord, it seems too good to be true. I can scarcely credit that it is possible." Hark how the everlasting hills echo and re-echo the assurance, "*It is possible! It is possible!*"

I suppose that there is nothing on earth so pure and white as the snow which comes quivering down from heaven, nor does anything look so dirty as the snow when once its virgin whiteness has been soiled. God made man in his own image, as pure and innocent and white as newly-fallen snow. Our first parents sinned, and we, following their example, added iniquity unto iniquity, and now each member of the human race is stained and polluted with a thousand sins. O God, in the wondrous chemistry of heaven is there anything that can make the snow that once was white as pure as ever? Yes, one thing, and only one—" *The blood of Jesus Christ his Son cleanseth us from all sin!*"

> " Helpless and foul as the trampled snow,
> Sinner, despair not, Christ stoopeth low
> To rescue the soul that is lost in its sin,
> And restore it to life and enjoyment again.
> His accents of mercy break soft on my ear;
> Is there mercy for me? Will he hear my poor prayer?
> O God, in the blood that for sinners did flow,
> Now wash me, and I shall be whiter than snow."

So much, then, for the exclamation, " If thou canst ! "

II. And now for the EXHORTATION, " Believe."

This command comes to every sinner direct from the Saviour. I invite you to trust Christ. I plead with you, I urge you. But there are times when Christian ministers must give up the persuasive, and, speaking with authority, command and exhort. " God commandeth all men everywhere to repent." " This is his commandment, that ye believe on Jesus Christ whom he hath sent."

At this good hour I bid you believe in Jesus if you have not yet done so. Let me take you through the story. Believest thou that God the Father sent his Son to be the Saviour of the world? Thou answerest, "Aye" to that. Thank God, for all men do not believe so much. Dost thou believe that he lived and died for sinners' sake, and bore their sins in his own body on the tree? Believest thou that he died *for thee?* I bless God for each that answers, " I do believe." But we must not forget our Redeemer's resurrection. On the third day he broke the bands that bound him, and shortly after soared aloft, leading captivity captive. Dost thou rejoice believingly in the resurrection of the Lord Jesus Christ—the proof and pledge that he had paid the sinners' debt to the uttermost farthing? "Aye, aye," say one and another. Praise God for that. But I want to know whether these matters are historically credited or personally trusted. It all hinges there. "Lord Jesus, I believe that thou didst come from heaven *for me*, as if there were no other sinner to be saved, that thou didst live and die for me, Thomas Spurgeon; and I believe that thou hast risen again to receive gifts for men, yea for the rebellious also, and that *I am one of the men*, for I certainly was a rebel." I charge you make a personal matter of it; for personal faith in a personal Saviour is what the Lord Jesus demands, when he says, "Believe, believe."

Did I hear some one remark, "If I am to be saved I shall be saved"? I am sure of that too. But if you are to be saved, you are to be saved in God's way, and that is, "Believe on the Lord Jesus Christ and thou shalt be saved." Suppose I want to find my way to London, and being a stranger in these parts I say to a passer by, "Can you tell me the way to London?" "Why," he says, "this road takes you there." "Oh," say I, "I am very glad to hear that." Straightway I sit down on the kerb, and when he asks me why I do not get away to London, I reply, "Didn't you tell me that this road takes me there?" Then he laughs at my folly, and says, "It does indeed take you there, if you walk along it, but you surely don't expect that it will carry you!" You smile at the illustration, but the ridiculousness of the supposition will, I hope, convince you that it is not even common sense for people to say, "If I am to be saved I shall be saved." Look you here, Christ Jesus is "*the way*, the truth, and the life." "He that believeth on him"—that is walking in the road—"is not condemned." "This is the way: WALK YE IN IT;" for Christ himself will not save you, cannot save you, unless you employ the means that he provides. In his name I again bid you trust your immortal soul, with all the sins of the past, and the present, and the future, in his mighty keeping. Lay hold on the Cross of Christ as Joab on the altar's horns, and rest assured that, sprinkled with the precious blood, you will remain happy, saved, and free.

"Oh but," says one, "mine is such a dreadful case—such a curious case." So was this poor boy's. The more reason thou shouldst believe, and believe at once. "But," says another, "I cannot believe unless God makes me believe, for is not faith the gift of God?" Yea, verily, but when God says "Believe," he gives us power to trust. I give my Master credit that he would not tantalize by saying "Believe," without enabling to do it—by giving a tonic to provoke appetite, and then refusing food to satisfy the cravings he himself caused. No. When he said to the man with the withered arm, "Stretch out thine hand," he helped him to do what till then was impossible, and it was restored whole as the other. And when he bade the ten men who were covered with leprous scales go and show themselves to the priests, he so arranged it that, as they ran, they should run away from the leprosy, nor did it ever catch them up again. When Joseph sent for his old father to come down into Egypt, he very properly provided some waggons to convey him with all his household stuff. And when God sends a message to me, saying, "Come to the Saviour," he sends me a chariot to come in, and gives me power to believe, for his people shall be willing in the day of his power. Be sure of this, that if the message comes to you, "Believe," you must believe, and you are able so to do.

Another reason why you should believe is this. Listen to it, for it is very solemn. *You will be damned if you do not.* That is God's own word. "He that believeth and is baptized shall be saved; but he that believeth not shall be damned." I heard my dear father say the other day in preaching that one of the most encouraging words for timid seekers was the word that I have just quoted to you, "He that believeth not shall be damned." I must confess that to me it was a new way of looking at it. But I soon saw his meaning, for he went on to say, "You cannot doubt your right to believe when God has said that if you do not believe you will be damned. You cannot keep on saying 'I am afraid that it was not meant for me and that I must not believe.' The dreadful penalty attached to unbelief makes that excuse impossible." Is it really so? Then, God helping me, I fling away my doubts. Here, Lord, I come just as I am, a poor, vile, guilty, helpless, ill-deserving, undeserving, hell-deserving worm. "If thou canst." No, I must not say that. "Lord, if thou wilt." No, it were blasphemy to suppose thee unwilling. "O Lord, thou canst save me: thou wilt save me: thou *hast* saved me. Glory to thy ever blessed name!" Oh, that you could come to that just now! Then this exhortation would not be in vain.

III. And now, briefly, on the last point—the EXPLANATION. "All things are possible to him that believeth."

I wonder which you think the best chapter in the Bible. My own mind is not made up yet. If I may have a choice it would light on any chapter that tells me about the sufferings of Christ. A joyful sorrow fills our hearts whenever we read the old, old story of Jesus and his love. But putting those chapters aside, and giving them pre-eminence, I think—well, there is the 14th of John, and the 3rd of John, and 23rd Psalm, and the 53rd of Isaiah—but I must not think of any more, yet I cannot forget the 11th of Hebrews, that wondrous record of the deeds of faithful men and women. I like to read that chapter as if I were walking through some grand cathedral with painted windows of the saints on every hand, and with the tattered banners of brave regiments hanging down the nave, while the organ peals out some martial melody as if it told the story of never-to-be-forgotten heroisms. Throughout the chapter we see the portraits of the saints; there hang the flags of faith that braved the battle and the breeze, while the heavenly music proclaims, "these all died in faith."

"All things are possible to him that believeth." Jericho, thy walls are very high and deep and strong, but they shall fall before the ram's horn of our faith. Rahab, thou art a harlot, but thy faith shall save thee for all that. Aye, and those who are destitute, afflicted, tormented, of whom the world is not worthy, shall obtain a good report through faith. Now, I believe—for God says it—that nothing is impossible to him that believeth. In this poor man's case it was his want of faith alone that prevented the immediate salvation of his child. The only hindrance, so far as I can tell, to the salvation of every one of you is the fact that you do not and will not believe in the Lord Jesus Christ. See, here is a vessel on the stocks, ready for launching. The shipwrights have long been at it. They have at last completed it, but it stands high and dry on *terra firma*. What is wanted to launch it into yonder river? Just one touch of a lady's finger upon the electric stop, and the ship shall glide down the ways, and walk the waters like a thing of life! God's Holy Spirit has worked upon some of you till you are almost ready—quite ready—for the launching, but on the stop of full decision your finger must be pressed, and you (not without help divine) must launch the vessel; in other words, you must have done with unbelief,—the dog-shore of mistrust, which keeps you on the stocks of indicision when you might be floating on the ocean of God's love, and serving the Lord with gladness of heart. "He could there do no mighty work," the record tells us of Jesus, "because of their unbelief." Let not this be true of your heart as of "his own country." The one thing needful is that you should trust in Christ. The sacrifice has been offered. The blood has been shed. The fire and smoke of the atonement have ascended to heaven. Our Surety and Substitute has been accepted by the Father, who first appointed him; and no more is needed for your salvation than that you should on your part accept the Substitute whom God approves. Your faith shall then become to you like Peter's angel, who, having roused him from his sleep, and burst the bonds of the prison-house, the huge door swinging open of its own accord, brought the apostle out into light and liberty and life.

> "Oh, believe the record true,
>   God to you his Son has given:
> You may now be happy too,
>   Find on earth the life of heaven;
>   Live the life of heaven above,
>   All the life of glorious love."

I thank God that it has been my lot to see some dreadfully wicked sinners saved. I do not believe in degrees of sin, mind you. I know that some of the best (so called) are amongst the worst. I mean that I have seen some whose hands have been dyed to the elbow with iniquity brought into light and life through Jesus Christ. Verily, there is nothing too hard for the Lord.

How well do I remember the happy days when my brother and I used to learn from our precious mother (God ever bless her), the way to heaven. On Sabbath evenings we stood beside her at the piano and sang the songs of Zion. Amongst the best of them was,—

> "There is a fountain filled with blood,
> Drawn from Immanuel's veins;"

and when we came to that beautiful chorus "I do believe and so on, mother used to say, "Now do not sing this if it is not really so with you. Do not let it be mere song on your part. Let me sing it alone unless you really mean it." And oh, how our little hearts used to break with longing for the day when each could sing for himself,

> "I do believe, I will believe,
> That Jesus died for me."

The day came at last to both of us—the happiest day that ever dawned on either him or me—and we have been able to sing ever since, despite our many faults and failings,

> "I do believe, I will believe,
> That Jesus died for me,
> That on the cross he shed his blood
> From sin to set me free."

We cannot have a better ending to this happy theme than the singing of a verse of that sweet hymn to the good old tune,

> "There is a fountain fill'd with blood,
> Drawn from Immanuel's veins;
> And sinners, plunged beneath that flood,
> Lose all their guilty stains.

May the Lord bless to us the preaching and the singing. Amen.

FINDING THE SAVIOUR.

"We have found him."—*John i.* 45.

THE Messiah had been promised long. Almost as soon as sin entered the world, and death by sin, the advent of the life-giving Saviour was foretold. It was eventide in the Garden of Eden, and behind some of the bushes our first parents had hidden themselves, for sin had made them ashamed, when a voice which they had loved to hear at other times sounded terribly in their ears. It was the voice of an angry God. How could he but be angry with these, who had just disobeyed his very reasonable command? "Adam, where art thou?" enquires the stern Deity, and the disobedient pair, taken almost in the very act, stand face to face with their accuser and their judge. They both with one consent began to make excuse. The man blamed the woman, and the woman blamed the serpent, and the serpent, I expect, would have blamed somebody else if there had been a chance. But or ever the crimson blushes had left their guilty cheeks, the promise that the seed of the woman should bruise the serpent's head shone like a dim star in that black night. Four thousand years passed by, with here and there faint glimmerings of the brighter light to come. The little star which shone in Eden's darkness was, doubtless, growing, though it twinkled with a feeble flame, and at times seemed almost quenched. The types and emblems of the Jewish dispensation, the songs and psalms of David, and the sayings and seeings of the prophets, served to keep the light alive. Then John the Baptist came. He was not that light, but was sent to bear witness of the light. "Coming events cast their shadows before them," and John was a luminous shadow from the Messiah, who was almost at hand. Then Jesus came, cradled in a manger where stalled oxen fed. He came from God's right hand, albeit he came as other children come—Son of God as well as Son of Mary. The promise given in Eden was fulfilled at Bethlehem four thousand years afterwards! The serpent's head was not yet broken, but the Breaker had appeared in the fulness of time. So Jesus came—the Saviour promised long. Say not he came with tardy footsteps, for he arrived as soon as God designed. For thirty years more the Champion tarried, till the time for baptism and public ministry had fully come. Then "he could not be hid," and John being one of the first to recognize him, did not hesitate to proclaim him, saying, "Behold the Lamb of God, which taketh away the sin of the world."

I have introduced my subject at such length that you may see how God designed to bring a blessing from the curse, and how, from the very earliest time of man's transgression, his heart was so full of love that he devised a scheme whereby Paradise Lost should become Paradise Regained. In accord with the simplicity of the text, we will have very simple divisions.

The text itself shall form the first. We will relate it as a joyous matter of fact that "*We have found him.*" The second point is, that *we want you to find the Saviour*—a very natural adjunct to the first. The third, that *there is no reason why you should not.* And the fourth, that *there is every reason why you should.*

I. WE HAVE FOUND HIM.

It ought to be, I think, a cause of some comfort to those who seek salvation to hear it recorded by so many faithful men and women that they have found the Saviour. Hope should rise immortal in their breasts when they hear of favours, the very favours that they seek, being distributed to their friends and fellows. For each may reason thus:—
"Well, if they have found Christ, why should not I? If they rejoice in Jesu's saving grace, may I not do the same? There is hope for me if there is hope for them; and since Jesus is the same yesterday, to-day, and for ever, as God is no respecter of persons, as it does not depend upon merit, but is all of grace, may I not venture to believe that I may yet be saved?"

Philip is the first to bear witness to the joyous fact that he has found the Saviour. He said it, I grant you, in a very literal sense, for his eyes gazed into the eyes of Jesus, and found them full of love-looks. Perhaps, too, he touched the person of our Lord. Jesus was visible and tangible then, and in a very emphatic sense the first disciples could say, "We have found him; we have found him." But, brethren, there are thousands of later saints who can say it just as positively, if not as literally. "*We* have found him." These outward eyes have never seen thee, Lord; my inside eyes have gazed upon thee, and I by faith am ever "looking unto Jesus"! I cannot touch thee, Lord, for thou art high and lifted up, yet I have come in contact with thee, and though I only touched the hem of thy garment, the touch has made me whole! And I have heard thee speak, Lord, for though no audible sounds struck my ears, a voice sounded in my heart to which my soul responded!

> "I see thee not, I hear thee not,
> Yet art thou oft with me,
> And earth hath ne'er so dear a spot,
> As where I meet with thee."

So we can say for ourselves as Philip did, "We have found him, we have found him, we have found him."

> "I've found the pearl of greatest price,
> My heart doth sing for joy,
> And sing I must, for Christ is mine,
> Christ shall my song employ."

Think of the thousands who are now in glory, who, if we could but hear their voices, would say to us, "We have found him; we have found him." The glorious company of the apostles cries, "We have found him, whose we are and whom we serve." The noble army of martyrs repeats, "We have found him; and though we waded through seas of blood for his sake, one sight of himself makes up for it all!" The hosts that have crossed the flood join in chorus with those who are crossing now, and heaven and earth take up the glad refrain of Philip, "We have found him; we have found him; we have found him whom our souls adore!" Is not the testimony of successful seekers encouraging to any sinner who still exclaims, "Oh, that I knew where I might find him"?

But what is it to *find* Jesus?

The phrase is so often used in religious conversation that it has become in reality a technical term, which, in spite of its simplicity, puzzles those who are "strangers from the covenants of promise." I do not know that I can do better than relate the experience of those who have found him. By nature we were without God, and therefore without everything, for God is everything. Without God, and therefore without hope in the world. Godless, and Christless, and hopeless! And we were careless, too—unconcerned about our dangerous condition. Through God's good Spirit we became at last concerned; our self-complacency turned into self-disgust; we loathed ourselves, and repented in dust and ashes. We saw that everything was not right. Nay, more, we saw that all was wrong, and then we took to prayer, and though we could not lift our eyes to heaven, and had to smite upon our breasts, we cried aloud, "God be merciful to us sinners." Oh, it is a blessed thing for any man when his self-satisfaction is shivered to a thousand fragments, and he begins to see himself as God sees him—a sinner, helpless, hopeless, and unsaved. The mariners, as they cross the sea, have a custom of putting a man on the very bows of the vessel to keep a smart look-out, and through the night, as the bells ring the hours, he shouts out how things are going on. Oftentimes in the stilly night, when sleep was wanting, we have waited for the tidings as if we enquired, "Watchman, what of the night?" and have rejoiced to hear the assuring cry, "All's well, all's well." 'Tis no small comfort, either, to hear those welcome words above the roar of the hurricane, and the clatter of the storm, "All's well, all's well." But there are some men who keep on saying "All's well" when it is anything but that. The storm does not affright them, and the dangers are not perceived. They cry peace, peace, when there is no peace. Better a thousand times would it be for them if in agony of soul they shrieked out, "Breakers ahead!" than that they should soothe themselves to slumber with "All's well" when really all's ill, for it must be ill with them until they exchange their self-righteousness for the better righteousness of the sinner's Saviour. It happened with some of us, that as soon as we found that we were wrong, we tried to set matters right ourselves, as if, forsooth, we could do without a Saviour. We soon discovered our folly; for the more we tried, the greater and more frequent were our failures. We found that there were rocks ahead, and so, as the sailors have it, we put the helm "hard over," in order to avoid them,—in other words, we effected a certain sort of reformation in our lives, changed our course a point or two, and it was well for us we did; but we soon discovered that there were rocks all round us, and that it was not in man to direct his way. We were hedged in round and about, and above and beneath, by the multitude of our transgressions. Then we also began to pray, for it was with us as with the mariners in the hundred and seventh psalm. When all their wisdom was swallowed up, then they cried unto the Lord in their trouble. Blessed is he who, having got to his wit's end, has still wit enough to look to the strong for strength, and to him who only can deliver. In answer to our earnest cry, we saw, dancing over the dreaded breakers, the twinkling light of the pilot's boat, and presently we hailed him aboard our storm-tossed barque. Then we cried aloud for very joy, "We have found him, we have found him." Since then he has been a pilot to our souls. He has guided us where we could not steer ourselves, and will yet bring us to the desired haven of everlasting peace.

The secret of true religion is to have found HIM. Some people find peace, but it is not worth finding, for it is only carnal security. Others, "get religion," which is very much like finding a block of quartz, and having no means of extracting the gold which may be in it. Religion is not Christ, though Christ is the sum and centre of true religion. It is himself we want.

"Give me Christ, or else I die!"

O blessed Master, I cannot be content until I clasp thee in my arms of faith, and say "I have found him, whom my soul loveth." Happy are they who, with the apostle Paul, count all things but loss for the excellency of the knowledge of Christ Jesus, their Lord, and are willing to suffer the loss of all things so that they may win Christ, and be found in him.

II. Secondly, having found Christ ourselves, WE WANT YOU TO FIND HIM. We are not amongst those who are afraid that heaven will be overcrowded, and that there will not be enough of breathing space. We say "The more the merrier," and our hearts rejoice to think of the teeming myriads—the multitudes that no man can number, joining in the song of Moses, and the Lamb. There are indeed some Christians selfish enough to congratulate themselves that they, and perhaps some of their nearest relatives and friends, are saved, without longing for the salvation of others. They remind us of him who is reported to have prayed, "O Lord, bless me, and my wife, my brother Bill, and his wife. Us four and no more, for Christ's sake. Amen." I must confess I can scarcely imagine any one praying so, the conclusion being specially objectionable. There could be no "Christ's sake" about such a petition, and how could any one say "Amen" to it? God would have all men be saved, and since he himself has opened the kingdom of heaven to all believers, we welcome all, saying, "Whosoever will, let him take the water of life freely." We cry to all, "Believe on the Lord Jesus Christ, and thou shalt be saved," and we rejoice to sing

> "I have a Father, to me he has given
> A hope for eternity, blessed and true;
> And soon will he call me, to meet him in heaven,
> But oh, may he lead you to go with me too!"

This longing for the salvation of the souls of our fellow-men is, after all, very natural. We can claim no credit for it. It must be with us as with the first finders of the Messiah. "One of the two which heard John speak, and followed him, was Andrew, Simon Peter's brother. *He first findeth his own brother Simon.* And he brought him to Jesus." It was so also with Philip, who, having been found of Christ, "findeth Nathanael, and saith unto him, We have found him." We are in the habit of recommending medicines that have done us good. Oh, let us get into the blessed habit of recommending Christ to sinners, and of leading them, as human instrumentalities best can, to the Saviour whom we have found to the joy and rejoicing of our hearts. If I may venture to alter the first line of a quotation from Miss Havergal, her sweet hymn will well express the desire I want to kindle in each Christian's breast.

> "I for myself have found him,
> Jesus is more to me
> Than all the richest, fairest gifts
> Of earth could ever be.
> And the more I find him precious,
> And the more I find him true,
> The more I long for you to find
> What he can be to you."

III. And now, thirdly, THERE IS—so far as I can tell—NO REASON WHY YOU ALSO SHOULD NOT FIND THE SAVIOUR. Is there any reason in Christ himself? "Well," says one, "if he were here in person it would be an easy matter. We would find him then, for we could track his footsteps; and when he said to us, 'Come and see where I dwell,' we could go as these early disciples did and spend the rest of the day with him." Ah, but, beloved friends, it was not seeing Christ's person, it was not handling Christ's body or his raiment, it was not hearing Christ's voice which saved these earliest converts. "Seeing is believing," says one. Believing is the very opposite of seeing, I reply. "We walk by faith, not by sight." True is it that John said, "Behold the Lamb of God!" but you do not think that one glance at his person took away sin. It was not so. It was as the beholders recognized in Christ the sacrifice—*the Lamb of God*—that their sins were taken away, although the offering was not yet complete. They were saved, as we are, by grace through faith, and that not of themselves; it was the gift of God. Christ's personal presence here might be a disadvantage, for we might fancy that simply seeing him and literally touching him would suffice. It is not sight, but FAITH that God requires. "Believe on the Lord Jesus Christ, and thou shalt be saved." If this be so, there is no reason in Christ, at all events, why you should not find him. You can see him now if but your eyes of faith are opened. He sits beside his Father in the exceeding glory, and—

"Looks like a Lamb that has been slain,
And wears his priesthood still."

Will you not exclaim believingly, "Thou art the Lamb of God. Thou hast died for my sins according to the Scriptures"? Believing this, you do indeed behold the Lamb of God, and he takes your sin away.

But is there any reason in yourself why you should not be saved? I know of none, except indeed your unbelief. Says one, "But I am so ignorant; I scarcely know the A, B, C." I am sorry for you, if that is so, but you may know the A, B, C of Christianity, though utterly ignorant of the alphabet of the spelling-book. Can you say your spiritual A, B, C? Repeat it after me if you can. A, is to "*Attend*" to the gospel, for "faith cometh by *hearing*, and hearing by the word of God." Do you attend to the gospel? Are you, like Lydia, who attended unto the things which were spoken of Paul? B, stands for "*Believe*," of course. "*Faith* cometh by hearing." The word does not profit unless it be mixed with faith in those that hear it. Do you believe that Jesus died for you, and that in his own body he bore your sins upon the tree? C, means "*Confess*," for "If thou shalt confess with thy mouth the Lord Jesus, and shalt believe in thine heart that God hath raised him from the dead, thou shalt be saved. For with the heart man believeth unto righteousness; and with the mouth confession is made unto salvation."

"But," says another, "I am so sinful." My dear friend, you are the very one to be saved, then—the very sort to find the Saviour, for your need is pressing, and your case is urgent. Moreover, Christ came not to call the righteous, but sinners to repentance.

And yet another says, indignantly, "But I am not sinful. I am a moral man, and I do this, that, and the other." I am very glad to hear it, my friend, but you need to find the Saviour for all that. Did you notice what we read about Nathanael just now? Christ himself said of Nathanael

"Behold an Israelite indeed, in whom is no guile." But there was one thing lacking—he had not found the Saviour till that moment, and all his guilelessness went for nothing; for a man may have no guile, and yet have plenty of guilt. I know not whether thou art guileless or not, but I do know that thou art guilty, for we all have sinned, and come short of the glory of God. The moral man, therefore, wants Christ as much as the immoral. "Talk we of morals? O thou bleeding Lamb, the best morality is love to thee!"

"Ah, but," another says, "any one may find Jesus—every one may find him but not myself. There is no mercy for me. I am shut up in the bondage and the darkness of despair." My dear friend, why not for you? It seems to me almost like blasphemy that any one should say that salvation is not for him. Why should you go down to the shore of the boundless ocean of God's eternal love, and draw a line across the golden sand, and say, "Hitherto shall the waves of God's redeeming grace come, but no further; and I am just beyond their reach"? You have no reason to suppose that you are out of the bounds of mercy. You are in them for certain if you will but believe on the Lord Jesus Christ, and give yourself, body, soul, and spirit, into the hands of a faithful Creator and a loving Redeemer.

IV. I have done when I have given a few reasons why you should be saved, for I think THERE IS EVERY REASON WHY YOU SHOULD FIND JESUS.

The first is, that *the gospel is preached in your hearing.* I can understand that the poor heathen, if they knew anything about it might say, "What hope have we? We never hear a gospel sermon;"—I speak of those to whom the light has not yet come—"we have no gospel privileges; the cross is not uplifted in our midst." But *you* do know the truth—

you have heard it over and over again ; and those of you who attend this Tabernacle have heard it as thousands of your fellow-creatures wish they could hear it, but do not get the chance, save through the printed sermons. What will you not have to answer for—you who have sat beneath the sound of a gospel preached as scarce another man in history has ever preached it? Is not this a great reason why you should find Christ? You will not have to search, as some do, through the labyrinths of ceremony and ritual. Jesus Christ hath been evidently set forth crucified among you ; and the cross, most beautiful because unadorned, is uplifted from this platform from Sabbath to Sabbath. You have glorious opportunities of finding Christ, for he is not hid ; he stands on this pulpit (if I may put it so), for the preacher preaches not himself, but Christ Jesus his Lord, and himself your servant for Jesus' sake. Here, then, the Saviour is to be looked at, to be loved, and trusted. "The word is nigh thee, even in thy mouth, and in thy heart ; that is the word of faith which we preach."

Another reason why you should find Christ is, that the proclamation of the word is seconded by *entreaty and persuasion of a private sort.* Some of you have had direct calls to God. You have lost some dear friend by death, or perhaps through some other cause which seems almost as grievous, for the friend is not dead, and yet is dead to you. Such things are God's knockings at your heart's door, and you have felt them. Christ has been just the other side of the door—so near and yet so far ! Perhaps it is so with you even now. What a glorious opportunity you have of finding him, for there is only the door of unbelief between you and him. Oh, fling the portals wide ! "Come in, thou King of glory ! Let the gates be lifted up, for thou art worthy to be received and honoured, King, Immanuel, Lord and Saviour!"

Is there not a longing with some of you for Christ? *You are seeking for him yourselves*, and this seems to me to promise well for your finding him; for when has he said to any of the seed of Jacob, "Seek ye my face in vain"?

The best hope of all is that *Christ is seeking you*. Beloved, not one of us would have found Christ unaided and unsought. While we were saying at the commencement of our meditation, "We have found him," I could hardly keep back the facts of the case which I have saved to the last. "We have not found thee, Lord, but thou hast found us." It comes to the same thing in the long run, but it is a very different thing, is it not? "If we did find thee, Lord, it was because thou didst draw us with the cords of love, and with the bands of a man." The prodigal found the father, but did not the father find the prodigal? "Jesus findeth Philip," so runs the record, and then Philip says to Nathanael, "We have found him." Truth to tell, there is in every case a blessed commerce between the two. He finds us, and then we find him. He loves us, and then we love him, for all the saints admit, "We love him because he first loved us."

Suppose you are at my father's house, and, having expressed a desire to walk round the garden, I tell you of some of the things that I would like you to notice, as I am unable to accompany you. For instance, I say, "There is a beautiful bed of roses which you must not miss." Then I give you some directions by which you may hope to find it; and yet you are by no means sure as to the exact locality. However, you go in the direction that I indicated, and presently you say to the friends who are with you, "Dear me, I think I smell some roses somewhere." And following the scent, you come upon the blushing beauties. On your return you say to me, "We found the bed of roses." Ah, but did you find the roses, or did the roses find you? Did not the roses send out their feelers of perfume to find you, as if to say "Here we are, waiting for you to come and admire us, waiting for you to delight in our fragrance"? You did not find the roses at all. Give them the credit of finding you. And thou, O Saviour, sweetest of the roses of Sharon, purest of the lilies of the valley, the savour of whose name is like ointment poured forth—thou hast come over the mountains of division, and with the breath of mercy drawn us to thyself! When we said that we had found thee, we really meant that thou hadst found us. All the perfume we have is thy perfume, for thou art to us as a bundle of myrrh; and all the grace that we possess is thine. Blessed rose of Sharon, we fasten thee to our hearts: we wear thee in our breasts, for we have "put on Christ." We fain would live as thou didst live, and gladly die, if needs be, for thy sake, thou fairest among ten thousand, thou altogether lovely One!

Oh, seek the Saviour—seek him with all your heart, and you shall assuredly find him, to the joy and rejoicing of your spirits. Pray God it may be so. Amen.

LYDIA AND THE JAILOR.

Acts xvi. verses 13 to 34.

YOU must have noticed before now the striking contrast between the conversions of Lydia and the Philippian jailor. It will be my endeavour, first to set these contrasts before you as strikingly as I am able, and then to show you that despite important differences there are, as there must be in all cases of conversion, certain points of resemblance which are deeply interesting. Our aim, then, is simply this, first to note how these cases differ, and next to remark the resemblances between them. In other words, we will contrast them, and compare them.

I. THE DIFFERENCES ARE MANY. The persons who were brought to a saving knowledge of the truth were counterparts of each other.

It is worthy of our notice, for instance, that *the grace of God was equally effective with either sex.* The woman of Thyatira and the man of Philippi were alike objects of redeeming love. In Christ Jesus there is neither male nor female, barbarian, Scythian, bond nor free. The grace of the Lord Jesus Christ is to all and upon all that believe, and all sizes and both sexes are influenced by his power to save. Some will have that the feminine character is particularly susceptible to the things of God,—that there is already a certain predisposition to religious exercises and influences, or at least a grace and tenderness of feeling which aids them in accepting the gospel in the love of it. I am afraid that the daughters of Eve are by nature as much the heirs of Satan as the sons of Adam, and that which is born of the flesh is flesh, still they have certain traits and characteristics which render them more pliable beneath the Master's hand, and more readily led by the grace of God. Do not misunderstand me. I must believe that nothing but the omnipotent grace of God can affect for good, even those who are most easily affected; nor is there in the sweetest character aught that can merit esteem, or give the Creator delight.

"The carnal mind"—whether it belong to male or female—"is enmity against God; for it is not subject to the law of God, *neither indeed can be.*" But is it not cause for joy when she who often goes by the name of "the weaker vessel" finds that Christ is indeed her strength,—that he is mighty to save,—and when the natural graces of her character are made still more graceful by the grace of God? Oh, that God would raise up in this land of ours, and in the colonies across the sea, faithful women who may become mothers in Israel and train their little ones in the fear of God! John Ploughman says very wisely, that "Samuel would never have been Samuel if Hannah had not been Hannah." How much depends upon the careful, prayerful, loving training which the little ones receive by their mother's side and at their parent's knee! I rejoice to read that Lydia was

Lydia and the Jailor.

brought to God, and that her womanly heart, with all its tender throbs and throes, was consecrated to a tender Saviour whose love and grace made her womanliness queenly, and taught her how to "love God and live for Heaven."

But what a mercy it is for mankind that God's grace is not confined to women! Alongside the story of Lydia's conversion is the history of the ingathering of the stern, sturdy jailor. Strong as man may be in mind and body—obstinate as he may be as to his hardened and unregenerate heart—there is something harder and something stronger. There is nothing so hard but a harder thing can get through it. Glass is not so hard but the sharp diamond can cut it. There is nothing too hard for the Lord; and the jailor's heart, seared and stiffened by his sin, can be broken by the mighty sledge hammer of the gospel truth. There is no sex as well as no sect in heaven, and even here in Christ Jesus we forget the differences, and the various drifts of mind and traits of character, influenced by the same Saviour's love, are consecrated to his praise while Christian men and women are bound up in the one bundle of life.

There is, however, a still greater difference in them in that *Lydia " worshipped God," and the jailor was a heathen.* We suppose that Lydia was a proselyte to the Jew's religion —that she worshipped the Lord God of Abraham and Isaac and Jacob, and though possibly born of heathen parents, she now saw that the gods of the heathen were no gods. So when she knelt in prayer, she lifted up her hands to God in the heavens, and when she sang, her hymns were directed to Jehovah's throne. Blocks of wood and stone were an abomination to her. The living and true God, with all that he had made, she adored and delighted in. The river that flowed beside her on that Sabbath afternoon served to remind her of God, "who sendeth the springs into the valleys, which run among the hills." In all about her she perceived a God who was wise and kind and faithful, nor could she help worshipping him, and blessing his holy name. Already the work of grace had begun within her soul, and God, having the key of mercy in his hand, was gradually opening her heart.

With the jailor things were very different. I do not know that he worshipped at all, or paid any vows whatever; but certainly he was without God and without hope in the world. The Romans did not select the best of men for jailors, for good men made bad jailors. They wanted men whose hearts were hard, whose spirits were unrelenting—men who would obey and more than obey the cruel sentence of an unjust judge—men who, like this one, having received such a charge, would thrust his guiltless prisoners into the inner prison, and make their feet fast in the stocks. If the Lord saves the jailor he will probably employ some extraordinary means, for his heart will not open to the key which unlocked Lydia's. Yet know you this—that the one is as easy to Omnipotence as the other. God can cut the stone out of the mountain's heart. He can draw Ephraim away from his idols. He can separate him from his sin, and make him yet to be a polished pillar in the temple of the Lord his God.

You remember that the jailor, when he thought his prisoners had escaped, was about to commit suicide. He had already drawn the sword. The glittering blade was at his throat when God Almighty took hold of his suicidal hand, as if he said to him, "O jailor, I want that throat of thine: it must sing my praises yet. The life which thou

Lydia and the Jailor. 45

art so ready to sacrifice, I claim as mine, and thou shalt
serve me as faithfully in days to come as thou hast served
the devil up till now." Thus did abounding grace overcome
the hardened sinner; the obdurate submitted to a power
divine, and he whose heart was like adamant yielded to
the love of Jesus. Here, then, are the respectable Lydia
and the disreputable jailor rejoicing in the sovereign love
that is no respecter of persons. Do any Lydias who have
already worshipped God, but have not come into the fulness
of the light and liberty of his children, read this? Or have
some jailors whose lives have been full of sin—who for aught
I know, have tried to kill themselves—glanced at this
sermon? Then come, Lydia, come, jailor—come just as
you are, for Jesus receives all and any.

> "Come, sinner, to the gospel feast;
> Oh, come without delay;
> For there is room in Jesus' breast
> For all who will obey."

You will find a great difference in the two as to the
circumstances of their conversion. Lydia was brought to a
knowledge of the truth *on the Sabbath Day*. Perhaps it
was a calm, beautiful Sabbath, warm enough to have the
prayer-meeting as usual by the river side. There it was
that Lydia found the river of the water of life. There she
heard and attended to the things which were spoken of Paul.
On that bright Sabbath Day the Lord himself put the
golden key into the wards of Lydia's heart, and, turning it,
took possession of her being. The Sabbath Day is pre-
eminently a day of salvation. When Jesus was in the flesh
he rested on the Sabbath Day, but his rest was holy service.
'Twas then he healed the man with the withered arm, and

made the blind to see, as if "the better the day the better the deed." "Good deeds have no Sabbath Day!"

The jailor, as you must notice, was saved *on a week day*. The difference, perhaps, is trifling in your opinion, but does it not all help to prove that places, and times, and circumstances need be no hindrance whatever to the saving power of God's grace? I have said that the Sabbath Day is pre-eminently a day of grace and salvation, and many of you have rejoiced to find it so. But there are many others who have found the Saviour on an ordinary day of the week, and why should it not be so? O blessed Master, we love to call this day the Lord's Day, but we do not mean by that that the other days are ours. Are they not all the Lord's days, and why should not men be saved on Monday as well as on Sunday? Why, indeed! for his grace abides the same yesterday (which happened to be Saturday), to-day (which happens to be a Sunday), and for ever—Monday, Tuesday, and Wednesday—all the days of the week, and all the weeks of the month, and all the months of the year, and all the years of our lives. Glory be to his holy name that time, and place, and date need not be considered in the matter of our salvation.

Suppose that on entering the house of a friend, he pushes towards me a large arm-chair, in which he bids me sit. I say to him immediately, "I won't sit there, thank you, I will take one of these smaller chairs. That arm-chair is yours." "Oh, yes;" he answers, "but they are all mine." He is quite right. All the chairs are his; but I was right too, for the arm-chair was his in a special sense, for there he was wont to sit. Now, all the days of the week are God's chairs, but the Sunday is his arm-chair (if I may put it so), in which he loves to sit to bless his people.

> The king himself comes near,
> And feasts his saints to-day;
> Here we may sit and see him here,
> And love, and praise, and pray."

This fact does not make the other days any the less his, nor render it impossible to seek and find his mercy in the very midst of the business and bustle of the week.

Notice, too, that *one was saved at mid-day and the other at midnight.* "The darkness and the light are both alike to thee!" While we are worshipping in England at the close of the day, our friends on the other side of the world, having finished their Sabbath, are wrapped in slumber, and while they were in the sanctuary we were sleeping. God's saving power was made manifest with them, I trust, though it was night with us, and it is being felt by us now though all is dark with them. And more than this. If he pleases, he can speak the word of power at dead of night and make the very visions win men to Jesus. God needeth not to see to save; he works as well at black midnight as in broad daylight. Indeed, he always sees, for there is no impenetrable curtain to him whose eyes are as a flame of fire. How thou wilt, and when thou wilt, O mighty Saviour, save, we pray thee, whomsoever thou wilt!

Note, also, that while *Lydia was saved at a river side, the jailor found liberty in a dungeon.* I should like to be converted by a river side. Shall I tell you why? Because I should find it, as Lydia did, so handy to the baptistery. Nor was the dungeon less convenient, though not so picturesque, for there was the prison bath-room ready to be used as a place of immersion; and there the jailor was baptized, "he and all his straightway." But I should certainly have preferred the river side for my spiritual birthplace. What a glorious place of worship it must have been—a natural cathedral, where the only pillars were the branching trees, and the only organ the ripple of the river's tide. O Lydia, we can almost envy thee thy happy lot! That was a sacred stream to thee indeed. Often didst thou wander by that same river on other Sabbath days, and call to mind the hour when first thy heart was opened by the Lord and rejoiced with joy unspeakable and full of glory. But, truth to tell, I would rather be saved in a lock-up than not saved at all. Though the jailor was converted in a dungeon, he was very soon brought out of the prison-house, for as soon as he believed he was "free indeed." What a Liberty Hall did that prison, deep, and dark, and damp, become! Every occupant of it was set free. Paul and Silas were released by the earthquake which God sent as his emancipator. All the prisoners were set free, for "every one's bands were loosed and all the doors were opened." Most wonderful of all, the jailor was liberated, for though he was the keeper of the prison he had been the greatest prisoner after all; the servant of his sin, the bond-slave of lust and passion and idolatry. He, and all his, step into light and life and liberty at the call of God.

> "Jesus the prisoners' fetters breaks,
> And bruises Satan's head;
> Power into lifeless souls he speaks,
> And life into the dead."

We will not choose the place in which to find the Lord. We only long to find him wheresoever he may be.

There are differences, too, as to the mode of conversion in each case. There are two methods of conducting a flock of sheep. One way is the Eastern style, in which the shep-

herd walks before his flock, calls the sheep by name, and
finds them running at his call. The other way is not half
so picturesque or gracious—driving the sheep, perhaps with a
stick, perhaps with a dog; but, indeed, so long as the sheep
reach the green pastures, it matters little whether they are
drawn or driven. If I might choose, I would rather be
drawn, but to arrive at the green pastures is the principal
thing. Am I not right in saying that *Lydia was drawn; the
jailor driven?* Yet they both could sing, as they tasted of
redeeming grace and dying love—

> " The Lord's my Shepherd, I'll not want,
>   He makes me down to lie
> In pastures green : He leadeth me
>   The quiet waters by."

Lydia's conversion was something like the opening of a
flower. The Lord opened her heart with the shinings of
his grace. His love to her was as the golden key of the sun
to the shut-up flower. See how the sleepy bud opens its
leaves, as if it stretched its arms on waking from repose, and
then looks up into the face of the sun to receive the blessings of the new-born day. Or it was with Lydia as when
the morning dawns, whereat the first few streaks of light
tinge the horizon and glint upon the hill-tops, and then the
sun appears, and gradually climbs its golden stairway till it
reaches the summit of its strength and floods the world with
light. So did the light break on Lydia's heart, for to her
who was "sometimes darkness" a light sprang up; then
she looked unto him and was lightened, and ere long she
rejoiced in the full blaze of the love of God. But the
jailor's conversion was in an altogether different style. It
was as sudden as Lydia's was gradual. It was as noisy as

Lydia's was serene. What matters it? God knows the best means to use, and use them he will to his own praise and glory.

The Philippian jailor is a firm believer in sudden conversions. I doubt not he is up there in glory, and if he could hold conversation with us he would gladly own that in a moment, in the twinkling of an eye, he literally leapt into liberty and praised God's saving grace.

Nor is the jailor alone in this matter. He who was once the dying thief has reason to rejoice through all eternity that salvation is not necessarily a matter of months and years. God works not by rule and rote and time. He can do in a moment what he may take a week, or a month, or a year to do. O God, to thee one day is as a thousand years, and a thousand years in thy sight are but as a single day. Well, Lord, whether by a gradual process, or by a *coup de main*, by the voice of Paul, or by the rush of the earthquake, so long as Lydia and the jailor are brought to thee, we will be well content, and thine shall be the praise!

These, then, are the differences. Let us praise God that they make no difference to him, and that he can save whatever the circumstances may be.

II. We turn now to notice SOME RESEMBLANCES BETWEEN THESE CASES. In the case of each, *salvation was the Lord's doing.* "Whose heart the Lord opened," we read of Lydia. She was a seller of purple, which was a royal colour; but while she sold purple, it was the Lord who wore the purple, for he proved himself monarch of her heart also. "Oh, but," says one, "you must not forget the favourable circumstances attending her case." Granted that there were such, I ask, "Who made the favourable circumstances?" Why, God himself, and none other. Some one remarks that a

Lydia and the Jailor. 51

certain vessel made a smart passage, because she had a fair wind; and another that God sped the ship. Just so, for it was God who sped the wind, whatever sped the ship. So, in this case, the circumstances which certainly favoured Lydia's ingathering were in the hand of God, as was Lydia herself. The fact that though "of the city of Thyatira," she was found at Philippi,—the fact that intent on worship she wandered by the river side,—the fact that Paul wandered there too, and that his words met her wants—all these were of God's arrangement, "Salvation is of the Lord." Nor can we doubt that it was God who brought the jailor to the feet of Jesus. Who sent that noisy earthquake to shake the dungeon's walls, and shiver the prisoners' chains, and burst the doors wide open? It was the voice of God that sounded. His hand heaved the earth and shook the foundations. So also was it the power Divine which broke the heart and brought tears to the eyes and softened the spirit of the hardened jailor. In either case it was the Lord's doing, and it was marvellous in our eyes.

In each case, too, *faith was exercised.* The apostle Paul spoke to the woman by the river side about Jesus. We are not told his text or sermon, but we are sure of his subject, for he had determined not to know anything among men save Jesus Christ and him crucified. He pointed Lydia to "the Lamb of God which taketh away the sin of the world." Her heart opened as she heard of the open heart of Jesus, and of the blood that was for sinners spilt. He spoke to her about Christ's death and resurrection; and Lydia attended unto the things which were spoken of Paul. She found herself exclaiming, "This Jesus of whom I hear shall be my Saviour—this Christ of whom the sermon tells shall be my Redeemer. I claim him as my own on this Sabbath afternoon. His death has brought me life, and his resurrection is the assurance that he has paid my debt to the uttermost farthing." And was it not through faith that the jailor received pardon and peace? Prostrate at the apostles' feet, he pleaded with clasped hands that he might learn the way to heaven, exclaiming, "Sirs, what must I do to be saved?" The only answer being, "*Believe* in the Lord Jesus Christ, and thou shalt be saved."

I care not who or what thou art, whether thou resemblest Lydia or the jailor, faith in Christ is the only way to God. They resembled one another, therefore, in that respect.

Were they not alike also in the matter of obedience? *Baptism followed in each case.* It was usual for converts to be baptized immediately on believing. It cannot be too soon after, for the Lord has joined faith and baptism together, and what God has joined together let no man put asunder! It was the joy of Lydia's heart to profess her faith in Jesus, and in the presence probably of the other women, to be immersed in the river which seemed to be flowing so near on purpose. And it was the jailor's delight to confess before the prisoners and his whole household his faith in the apostle's Master, as he was immersed according to Christ's command in the name of the Father, and of the Son, and of the Holy Ghost.

A very pleasing resemblance consists in the fact that in each case *the families were included* within the saving grasp of the mighty hand of Jesus. It is very evident from the context that Lydia's household believed, and we are told distinctly that they were baptized. I know not if there were any children there; but if so they were old enough to receive the truth, and to understand the ordinance. And with the jailor it was very similar. The mother, and children, and servants, followed where the father led. Thank God, it is often so. Would God it were always so. As soon as the jailor believed, Mrs. Jailor gave her heart to Jesus, and all the little Jailors too; and they were forthwith baptized, he and all his, straightway. They did not wait to have the water warmed, nor specially to attire. Obedience is twice as sweet for being ready and immediate. In each case, then, they all believed alike, and were baptized at once. One of the greatest inducements for fathers and mothers to become Christians is the hope that by so doing their households will be brought to God. Have you not heard the story of him who climbed the precipitous hill—so steep that he had to cut his pathway up the cliff? He was followed by his son, whose voice he presently heard saying, "I am coming, father." And, oh, how carefully he picked his way then, lest, following in his footsteps, his boy should fail to go where he succeeded in scrambling his dangerous course! Think of that, father: your boy is coming after you; think of that, mother: your girl is just behind you; and in your footprints the child will probably tread; and the chances are—the blessed hope is—that if you believe in God with all your heart, your house will do the same, and you will stand at length before the great white throne, and with a heart overwhelmed with joy, will have to say, "Here, Lord, am I, and the children which thou hast given me."

It is pleasing to notice, too, that in each case *gratitude for their salvation showed itself* in deeds of kindness to the instruments. Lydia was no sooner converted than she said to Paul and Silas, "I wish you would come and stay with me for a few days. I will make you as comfortable as ever I can. I do not like you going from pillar to post. You have done my soul good, and I want to do your bodies good. You have been the saving of me and of my house; and now, if I can feed you and help you in any way, come, and I will give you board and lodging, and you shall have the best I have got." There they tarried till taken to jail, but again found a refuge in her home when they went out of the prison. Well done, Lydia! And yet it was no more than she ought to have done, for gratitude to God and gratitude to God's agents must result, if saving work has been truly accomplished. How was it with the jailor? He changed from a fiend into a ministering angel; the lion became a lamb! He who thrust the prisoners into that damp, dark, dismal, hole, unfit for a dog's kennel, with all their stripes still red and raw, and screwed their feet into the stocks, now gets basins and sponges to wash their stripes withal. And though it was dead of night, he brings them into his own house and gives them either a very late supper or an early breakfast. How could he do otherwise? for through them he and his had found the Pearl of great price, and now his grateful heart will take every opportunity, not only of blessing God directly, but of showing kindness to his servants.

Oh brother, sister, if thou art truly on the Lord's side thou lovest the Lord's people. Thou wouldst do anything for Jesus; a stripe is never so sore and uncomely but thou wouldst wash it; and a task is never so menial and paltry but thou wouldst do it gladly for Jesus' sake.

The last point of resemblance is by no means the least. They have each arrived to *the same glorious heaven!* Oh, is it not a blessing to know that there is only one heaven? "What do you mean by that?" says one. I mean exactly what I say. There is only one heaven, and we shall

all be together there, and all on an equal footing. I do not
say but that, as stars differ from each other in glory, so we
may shine with various lustre. But I know that we shall all
be "accepted in the beloved," that we shall all be "one in
Christ Jesus;" and if there are any differences, there will
be no divisions. I am quite sure of that. What think
ye—that there are first, second, and third class in glory? It
is all first class in heaven, and we shall all be there in the
same compartment, seeing the face of the same dear Redeemer, singing the same song of Moses and the Lamb,
and enjoying for ever the treasures and pleasures of God's
infinite grace. I like to think that the jailor, with all his
roughness gone, is near to the Saviour's heart, and that
Lydia, naturally soft and amiable in her character, is
now as near as can be to the selfsame fount of love. O
happy Lydia, thy halcyon days have now begun! It was
sweet for thee on earth to walk beside the Philippian stream
—to wander beneath the shades of the trees which grew by
that river's bank; but thou art happier now. Sin cannot
touch thee now, for thou hast reached the place where *praise*
is wont to be made; and now the river by which thou wanderest is the river of the water of life which breaks from the
throne of God; and the trees beneath whose shade thou
dost recline are none other than those wondrous trees of
life whose manner of fruit is twelve! Blessed art thou,
Lydia, having exchanged earth for heaven; the joys that are
here for greater joys above; and all the sorrows of earth for
the undimmed, unspoiled happiness of eternity!

And how fares it with the jailor? Ah, there is no midnight in that city, for "the Lamb is the light thereof." And
there are no earthquakes there, for there is no earth to
quake, and heaven cannot tremble, for it is a city that

hath foundations whose builder and maker is God. And there are no dungeons and prisoners there! It is the land of liberty and life: the only chains are chains of eternal love. Thou art shut in again, O jailor, more securely than thy prisoners were, but thy residence is the palace of the King!

> "Far from a world of grief and sin,
> With God eternally shut in."

Look up, beloved friends. Pierce ye the clouds with eyes of hope and faith, and behold sweet Lydia and her loved ones there with the jailor and his family. Nay, forget that they are there, and see the Saviour only. That shall be my heaven—to gaze upon my Maker's face, my Master's form, my Saviour's scars. O Lord, earth might be heaven; the Philippian dungeon might be heaven, if thou wert there; and heaven itself might be a dungeon—no, it might be hell, if thou wert elsewhere.

> "Thy shining grace can cheer
> The dungeon where I dwell:
> 'Tis Paradise when thou art there;
> If thou depart 'tis hell."

Blessed Master, we are coming to thee. Fast as the days roll by, we are hastening home; and, better still, thou art coming to us. Even so, come: come quickly, Lord Jesus. Let every Christian heart exclaim, "Amen." The Lord bless you for his mercy's sake! Amen.

COMING TO JESUS.

"Him that cometh to me I will in no wise cast out."—*John* vi. 37.

IT is a common expression that everything is easy when we know how to do it. The geography of countries and cities is plain when one has travelled round the coasts and traversed the streets. Things which are mysterious before we come into actual contact with them become as plain as possible when we investigate them. Some of the truths which are plainest and simplest to the children of God are most puzzling to those who are not Christ's. Having trusted Christ for ourselves we call faith an easy matter. We have already come to Jesus, and the geography of Calvary and Mount Zion is understood by us. But, until we did come into actual contact with Christ, we did not know what faith in Jesus meant; and until we quitted for ourselves the City of Destruction, habited in the pilgrim's garb, we were strangers to all the facts and experiences connected with the pilgrimage to the New Jerusalem. So is it with those who are still in nature's darkness. Our ordinary expressions are unintelligible to them; nor is it to be wondered at. The things we speak of are spiritual, and must be spiritually discerned. "The natural man receiveth not the things of the Spirit of God, neither can he know them, because they are spiritually discerned." However simple may be our language, the spirit of it remains uncomprehended and unapprehended by those who are still of the earth and earthly. Yet we must speak simply to sinners about the way to heaven, in the hope that light may break in upon them. We shall indeed do well, oftentimes, to simplify simplicity, to explain our explanations, and, having pointed out the way, ourselves to travel with them, that we may show them as well as speak to them about the way of life.

I have already spoken about "Finding the Saviour," our text being, "We have found him;" but I must travel on the same rails again, taking another very ordinary expression as the basis of our meditation. Coming to Jesus, then, is our theme.

Our divisions shall be these: First, *What is coming to Christ?* Secondly, *Who may come?* And, thirdly, *What if we do come?*

I. First, then, WHAT IS COMING TO CHRIST?

We often get a very clear idea of a fact by hearing the opposite of it. In other words, a negative demonstration is often more forceful than a positive one. If this be so, let me tell you what coming to Christ is not.

It is not coming to church. We have an old phrase, "The nearer the church the farther from God;" and I am afraid that it is very often true. The house of Justus joined hard to the synagogue, and its owner seems to have been just in character as well as by name, for he worshipped God and befriended the apostles; but there are some whose houses "join hard to the synagogue" who are still far off from God by sin and wicked works. We may dwell in the house of God—aye, and minister in it, and yet, like Eli's sons, be castaways. Nor does coming to Christ consist in the observance of ceremonies and ordinances. "I have been confirmed," says one. And what good has that done thee, my friend, if thou hast never trusted Christ? for there are, walking in our streets and drinking in our public-houses, men and women who have been confirmed, and some of them are confirmed drunkards now. "Ah, but," says one, "I have already effected a reformation in my character; and is not that coming to Christ?" Nay, verily, there is as much difference between reformation and salvation as there is between a reformatory and a palace. Says another, "I have reached that state in which I find a continual improvement in myself; and I am hoping that by careful consideration and judicious conduct I shall yet perfect myself in all manner of godliness." Well, so far thou hast done well to improve thyself, for, God knows, there was room for it; but until thou hast come to Christ, thy living, loving Saviour, improvement is, after all, little worth the having. Men have improved themselves into hypocrites,—improved themselves into all manner of unrighteousness by reason of their self-righteousness,—improved themselves at last to the mouth of the pit; and unless they came at last to Christ it swallowed them up quick, improvement and all. No; all depends upon that little word in our text, "Me." "Him that cometh to *me*, I will in no wise cast out," for until I have got right up alongside Christ Jesus, and, with my namesake, Thomas, have put my hand within his open side and clasped his feet and said, "My Lord and my God," I have not come to anything worth the coming to, for Jesus is the only Saviour of my soul.

Well, then, what is coming to Christ? Christ is a Saviour. A Saviour from what? "Thou shalt call his name Jesus, for he shall save his people *from their sins*"! If this be so, no one will come to the Saviour until he has first perceived that he is a sinner. The first item, then, in a definition of "coming to the Saviour" is *a sense of sin*. No man will go to a physician, I take it, until he discovers that he is sick. There are, indeed, some forms of disease so dire and terrible that the patient fancies he is well and stands not in need of medicine; but as soon as he finds out his sickness he has already begun to come to the physician. It is the earliest step, the first move in the right direction. Therefore coming to Christ is, first of all, having a sense of sin.

But, strange to say, a sense of sin—a consciousness of guilt—is one of the very last things to trouble a man unless his state is revealed to him. You meet a drunkard, for instance, in the street, who by his very look and walk proclaims himself to be intoxicated. I venture to assert that, if you tell him he is drunk, he will declare that he is nothing of the kind, and probably protest with oaths that he is a Blue-Ribbonite. The fact of the matter is that sin is hardening and blinding in its effects. It is possible that the drunkard honestly imagines that he is a sober man, for he has so far got off his head and lost his senses that he does not know what he is, and cannot be an impartial judge of himself. What is true of drunkenness is true, in its degree, of every other sin. Many sinners accused of guiltiness indignantly deny the charge. They are at least as good as other men, and a great deal better than some. Thus, O God, we feel that what we want at the very outset is to see ourselves as thou seest us—to look within, the candle of the Lord being our light in that dark place, that we may discover what a cage of unclean birds the best of human hearts is, and that we may then come to thee by way of Jesus, for thou alone canst put the wrong right and cause us to rejoice in holiness ! It is essential that the sinner shall see himself to be a sinner before he comes to the Saviour. The prodigal must come to himself before he arises to go to his father. You must cry "Show me myself" before you pray "Show me thyself." Nor will it suffice to see your sin ; *you must come to hate it.* It is one thing for me to discover that I am loathsome ; it is another thing for me to loathe myself and to repent in dust and ashes. It is well when I find out that I am helpless; but that is not enough. I must be sorry for the sin that made me helpless, and repenting before the living God, determine to slay the sin which nailed my Saviour to the accursed tree. It is possible to perceive sin and to remain in it. What we want is to see the sin and abominate it,—to flee from it as Lot out of Sodom, and not to look back upon it like the patriarch's wife. There must be no halting between two opinions ; but as soon as we discover that Baal is a false god we must run to the true God, and not go limping, as the Israelites did, betwixt the two. "How long halt ye between two opinions?" If the world and the flesh and the devil are worthy your consideration and concern, abide by them, hold to them, and spend and be spent in their service. But if God be the true God,—if Christ be the loving Saviour of mankind,—if his religion is true and himself the Truth,—then be a Christian out and out. But to go limping like a halt man, first to the one and then to the other, is out of all consonance with what is faithful and right and true. First, see your sin ; then hate it ; and then flee from it as a man flees from a venomous serpent. Speaking of serpents, reminds me of an act that a little boy in the colonies once performed, which may serve as a lesson to all who find out the hatefulness and the hurtfulness of sin. Being bitten in the finger by a snake, and knowing that, sooner or later, he must pay the death-penalty, he rushed to his home, seized an axe, and, laying his bitten finger on a block, severed it from the hand; for it was better for him to enter into life minus one of his members than, having the virus in his veins, by-and-by to perish. O God, I have been bitten by that old serpent, the enemy of my soul, and, having discovered, through thy grace, that I am poisoned through and through, I fain would lose my right hand,—lose everything, if I may but win Christ, whom to know is everlasting life! Sin is so hateful and harmful that we may well long to be rid of it, and be content to part with things most precious that are poisoned by it. Oh, to hate it as God hates it—to hate it so much that no sacrifice will be reckoned too great if but its venom may be vanquished!

Coming to Christ, then, includes a sense of sin, and a consequent hatred of it.

But these are only two steps towards a third. *Appreciation of Christ as a Saviour* must follow—an appreciation that induces appropriation. It is not enough for me to find out my nothingness: I must discover Christ's everythingness. It is not sufficient for me to know that I am sinful: I must find out that Christ is my Saviour. I shall be plunged into despair if I look only on the dark picture of my own worthlessness; but if a view of his righteousness dawns upon me, forthwith a star has risen which gives me hope, and leads me, with the Eastern Sages, to the place where Jesus is. On reaching him, and trusting in him, I find my sins removed and all my faults forgiven.

Christ's own definition of coming to him is the best that I can give you. He speaks, in the chapter from which our text is taken, of hungering and thirsting, and eating and drinking, and believing. If you read the chapter carefully, you will find that these terms are synonymous with each other. To come to Christ is to believe in Christ, just as to eat of him, or to drink of him, is to believe in him. He himself uses terms that are commonest amongst us, such as eating and drinking, and coming and finding. And, since he himself has spoken so, I cannot do better than to repeat over and over again his words, "Come unto me all ye that labour and are heavy laden, and I will give you rest." "If any man thirst let him come unto me and drink." "He that cometh to me shall never hunger, and he that believeth on me shall never thirst." To come to a physician is to seek his aid, to take his medicine, to adopt his principles, and to abide by his commands. To come to Christ is to believe that, sick as we are, his word can heal us; that, evil as we are, his righteousness can clothe us; that, hell-deserving as we are, his grace can pluck us from between the very bars of the fire, like brands from the burning, and cause us at last to shine as stars for ever and ever. O bleeding Lamb of God, I cannot stop away from thee! Thou art my only Saviour, my only refuge, the alone hope of my shipwrecked soul!

> "Lo, glad I come, and thou, blest Lamb,
>   Shalt take me to thee as I am.
> Nothing but sin to thee I give:
>   Nothing but love shall I receive."

Such is coming to Christ. Oh, that you may be led to come!

II. Now, secondly, WHO MAY COME TO CHRIST? The

question, I think, is answered in our text, for Christ says, "*Him* that cometh to me I will in no wise cast out." Somebody asks me, "To whom does that '*him*' refer?" I answer your question by asking you one: "To whom does not that '*him*' refer?"—for I think that is the better way to put it. You say, "Whom does it mean?" I say, "Whom does it not mean?" for it seems to me wonderfully inclusive. All the world and his wife may come in that. "Him that cometh I will in no wise cast out." O Saviour, how couldst thou have thrown the door more widely open than that? Nay, thou hast lifted the door from its hinges, and taken the door-posts away as well, and opened the kingdom of heaven to all believers, for "*Him* that cometh to me I will in no wise cast out." How was it in the life of Christ? Did he send any empty away? They came to him from every quarter, and they were all sorts and sizes and sexes; but not one of them did he refuse. There were soldiers, and sailors, and tax-gatherers, and physicians, and Pharisees, and scribes, and harlots, and thieves. I cannot continue the list. There were some of every sort, and each received his mercy, and tasted that the Lord was gracious. If you ask me, Who *will* come? that is quite another matter, though that also is answered in our text. "All that the Father giveth me shall come to me." Right blessed "*shall*"! And so they shall, for having been given to thee, O Saviour, by the hand of one who cannot make mistakes—their names already written on thy heart, and graven on the palms of thy hands—to whom else could they go? All, too, whom the Father gives must be drawn, for Christ himself said, "No man can come to me except the Father which hath sent me draw him."

Coming to Jesus.

I imagine that some one in this congregation would like to say to me, "But how do you reconcile those two things? Here is Christ saying, 'Let anybody come and I will receive him;' and yet in the same break he declares that only those can come whom the Father draws, and who have been already given to the Son." My dear friends, I do not see the need to reconcile them. God's word is true. "Let God be true, and every man a liar;" and, if they do seem to contradict each other, let them seem to contradict, though, indeed, to me it is not so. I do not see that they are at variance the one with the other. I am sure that I have been given to the Son, because I have come; and I was most certainly drawn, for I should not have come else. And you who have not come can be sure that you have been given only by coming. That is God's way of proving the fact to you. You want to find it out by some other plan. You want to go round by the back way and see into the secrets; but the Lord says, "Knock at the front door, and you shall be let in." He has every right to put it so, and to claim from us our faith in the Lord Jesus Christ without any further promise than that the faith shall be honoured and the sinner saved.

Man's responsibility and the sovereignty of God's choice are not at variance one with the other. They are distinct and separate, I grant you. They do not coincide, but there is no collision. Keep them separate—render to God the things that are God's, to man the things that are man's, and you will come to believe if you cannot fully understand that he who has compassion on those on whom he will have compassion, is perfectly honest and gloriously consistent when he cries aloud to all the world, saying, "Him that cometh to me I will in no wise cast out."

The natives of Australia were very much surprised the first time they saw a man on horseback. They had seen a horse before, and they had seen a man before, but they had never seen a man and a horse together before. They fancied that some unheard-of monster was coming upon them, which in the distance looked like a gigantic emu. But when the apparition drew near, and they perceived that the creature resolved itself into man and horse, their fears were allayed. The reason why the doctrines of Divine sovereignty and human responsibility appear so inconsistent to some is, that they are not regarded as quite distinct: the one being as far above the other as man is superior to the horse. They were made to go together, though they can never be one. No one would think of reconciling steed and rider. Seek not to reconcile these doctrines. Give each its proper position, and grace and wisdom appear, instead of inconsistency and partiality. Assign to God the honour that is due to his name, and the right to choose and to refuse, and at the same time feel that thou thyself art answerable for all that thou dost or dost not do. Then, and only then, the mystery is solved. "He doeth according to his will in the army of heaven, and among the inhabitants of the earth: and none can stay his hand or say unto him, What doeth thou?" At the same time, every man is intelligently responsible, and, since faith in Christ is the ordained way of life, it is for each to come to Christ and trust in him, thereby proving that they are ordained unto everlasting life.

We fall back on the invitation, Christ says, "Come, come, come unto me." The gospel is in that word "come." It is the gospel in miniature,—the gospel condensed. "COME." How often it appears throughout the sacred page. Christ is always saying it in different forms. He says it so often because he means it so fully. When you want to bring your child in from the street or garden, you say, "Come, come, come, come, come," as quickly as ever you can, do you not? And the repetition and the earnestness of the voice seem to intimate to your child that you are anxious for him to come, and that at once. That is just how Christ talks to us, "Come, come, come, come," he says. "All ye that labour and are heavy laden, come." "Ho everyone that thirsteth, come." "Let him that is athirst, come. And whosoever will, let him take of the water of life freely." I bless God for this sweet word, "come"—the beckoning finger of the Deity which summons me to heaven,—to peace and pardon here, and into full fruition there. "Come" is the key-note of the gospel, the master-tone struck from the sweet instrument of sovereign mercy. Let us hear it over and over again; it is sweet on earth, and oh, how sweet it will sound when the Master says, "Come up higher," and when at the pearl-built gates, with outstretched arms and open heart he cries, "Come in, come in, thou blessed of the Lord: come in, come in!"

> "Still shall the keyword ringing,
> Echo the same sweet, 'come';
> Come with the blessed myriads
> Safe in the Father's home.
>
> "Come, for the toil is over;
> Come, for the feast is spread;
> Come, for the crown of glory
> Waits for the weary head."

If you ask me, Who may come? I answer, All may come, for everyone is invited.

III. And now, lastly: WHAT IF I DO COME? I have undertaken a very great responsibility, for I have been urging you to take a certain course; and if you take it and find yourselves disappointed, you can visit your chagrin upon my head. I feel, dear friends, that I have been telling you something of the deepest importance; and eternal woe is mine if I have told you untruthfully and pointed you amiss. Some people come to me and others write about emigrating to New Zealand, and I feel the responsibility of advising them; for if, on arrival, they fancied that things were not exactly as I had led them to hope, they would not have very kindly feelings towards me. I therefore hold my peace as much as possible, and speak with bated breath and cautious language when urged to advise. But I do not hesitate to speak about coming to Christ, for I have tasted the Lord is gracious, and am sure that disappointment is impossible. Loth as I may be to prophesy about your prospects in the colonies, I am ready and eager to recommend you to emigrate to Jesus and throw in your lot with the people of God. Nay, I fain would conduct you to the Saviour, as Andrew did Simon. Knowing something of the Land of Promise, the heavenly Canaan, I advise you by all means to come. You will improve your condition wondrously. You will better your position a thousand times. Christ's wages are generous, his bounty boundless, his love inexhaustible, and himself most glorious. "O Lord God of Hosts, blessed is the man that trusteth in thee!" We who have come to Jesus and received his blessing say unhesitatingly, "Seek ye the Saviour too."

But perhaps you are not willing to rely upon our experience. Then I will put it this way: *you will not be worse off* for trusting Christ than you are without faith in him,

Think of your present position. You are without God, and therefore "without hope in the world." If you trust in Christ and find that you are hopeless still, you will be only as you were. My brother, if thou believest not in the ever blessed Son of the living God, thou must be lost eternally. Now, suppose that our religion and most holy faith are all a fraud and failure, thou canst but be lost. Hell's fires will be no hotter for thy faith in Christ, and the eternal burnings no longer for thy trust in Jesus. Putting the matter on ground which I hardly like to use, I press upon you the fact that if you make up your mind to love and fear and serve God henceforth, instead of serving yourself and living in sin and doing the devil's work, you are not running an awful risk of ruining your prospects or losing your soul.

But consider: *You may be better off.* Come, you will grant me this. There is a possibility of mending your position, is there not? You have heard, surely, of some who have lived happy lives ever since they trusted Christ. Though they have had their sorrows, they have had joys on the top of their sorrows: so much so that they have been able to sing in the fire and to shout in the furnace. And you have heard of some—perhaps you have known and loved them— who have died triumphantly, and passed through the gloomy valley, to find that it was hardly gloomy, as the light of God seemed to leap over the hills, and turn round the corners, and cause the very darkest places to be flooded with glory-light. Well, then, if that has been so with some, it may be so with you. There is a bare chance, a mere possibility, surely, you will grant me that.

Well, then, run the risk, if risk there be. You are prepared to run risks in business and social matters.

> "Oh, make but trial of his love:
> Experience will decide
> How blest are they, and only they,
> Who in our Christ confide."

My last point is: If you will trust in Christ, or "come" to him, as he puts it, *he will receive you.* Experience makes me sure of this. There are hundreds amongst us who have come to Jesus—who have forsaken every hope except the hope that is in Christ—who have given up all for the Saviour, and are glad of it. It was the best day's work they did. Their greatest losses have been their richest gains. They were never so rich as when they found themselves rich in faith. The experience of others, surely, ought to prompt you to try for yourselves. There is a custom, so they tell me, with the beggar men in this great city, to make marks on the door-posts of the houses which they visited, to tell their brethren who are sure to come after them whether it is worth their while to beg there. If a mendicant obtains relief, I do not blame him for making a scratch on the outside gate-post, which says to those who can read the hieroglyphic, "It is worth your while to go down that drive, though it is a long one, for you will find a welcome at the end of it." But I should feel inclined to blame a hungry outcast who, having deciphered that sign should say, "Well, I do not know. I do not think it is any good to go so far down to the house. It is too long a walk and too much of a chance," and then leave as famished as ever. He deserves to go without, for his predecessor's experience should assure him that he might get ample reward for the journey. On the door-post of the mercy-house of God I find inscribed by one who begged before me, "Thou, Lord, art good and ready to forgive." "This poor man cried, and the Lord heard him." And Paul has put his mark upon the gate-post, too, for he has written, "This is a faithful saying, and worthy of all acceptation, that Christ Jesus came into the world to save sinners, of whom I am chief." Oh, come, come, beggars as you are, to the Palace of Mercy, to the House of Bread. Here is bread enough and to spare, made of the old corn of the kingdom, and here are wines on the lees well refined.

> "A Saviour kind, a gracious God,
> A wardrobe rich and rare,
> A crimson bath of precious blood,
> Are waiting for you there."

Christ's own word, too, ought to assure you of his power and willingness to save you. The Master has come and is calling for you. He calls in words of such assurance that I wonder how you doubt him. He who cannot lie says plainly, "Him that cometh to me I will *in no wise* cast out." "I will not, I will not cast him out;" for the original runs very strongly. You cannot make it read too emphatically. You may crowd the phrase with "nots" and noes and it is still none too good to be true. "Him that comes to me I will not, no, I will not cast out."

O blessed Master, if there were not a saint on earth to bear witness to the verity of thy statement,—if everything seemed to say that it was false, I would accept thy word, for thou hast said so positively, so persuasively, that thou wilt cast none away! I must not, cannot doubt thee! I come to thee just as I am. Oh, pardon me, my Lord, for thy sweet mercy's sake! Go and do likewise, I beseech you.

> "God loved the world and sent his son
> To drink the cup of wrath;
> And Jesus says he'll cast out none
> That come to him in faith."

One word, and I have done. Some time before I left the other side of the world, where God has called me to preach this same gospel, I received from home a very beautiful Christmas-card, which I greatly prize, partly because it is most artistic in itself, but more because of the good mother who sent it to me. Across a troubled sea, angry and storm-tossed, a sea-gull flies with its snowy wings outspread above the dark waters, its whiteness standing in striking contrast to the gloomy clouds, while just above the picture are these words: "I would take thee home to my heart, but thou wilt not come to me." I am not ashamed to confess that, when I read the inscription, the tears started to my eyes, and I said to myself, "O mother mine, how gladly would I come to thee if I only could!" But on my voyage home—for the way soon after opened for me to return—I occupied some of my leisure moments in making as exact a copy of this picture as I could. The same white sea-bird, the same angry waves, the same dark clouds; but I did not put the same words above them. I sent the sketch on from Naples, so that it might arrive before me some four or five days, and this was the message that it brought: "I am coming home to thy heart! Wilt thou not welcome me?" The answer I received at ten o'clock one Thursday night, when mother's arms were round her son and mother's kiss was on his lips.

O God, how often hast thou said to the prodigal, "I would take thee home to my heart, but thou wilt not come to me." Oh, help him now, as thy Spirit only can, to say believingly, "I am coming home to thy heart! Wilt thou not welcome me?" Oh, that thou wilt! So let it be for thy mercy's sake. Amen.

A WHITE STONE.

"To him that overcometh will I give to eat of the hidden manna, and will give him a white stone, and in the stone a new name written, which no man knoweth saving he that receiveth it."—*Revelations* ii. 17.

ENQUIRY and speculation as to the exact meaning of some references contained in this text will not greatly profit us. It will be far better to take a bird's-eye view, if I may put it so, of a passage which seems rather remarkable at first sight; then prayerfully and longingly to gaze into it until the different figures and subjects stand out from the canvas.

The first thing that strikes us in this text is *victory*, "To him that overcometh," and that shall be our first division. The second point is *purity*, for we read about a white stone. The next is *novelty*, for "a new name" is promised. The fourth is *secrecy*, for no one knows the name save he that receives the stone. The last point shall be called *charity*, for the Spirit saith that to him that overcometh will God *give* to eat of the hidden manna; the white stone is also *given*.

I. VICTORY. "To him that overcometh." There is before my mind's eye a vision of the ancient Olympic games. There is the vast amphitheatre, with seats rising tier on tier, crowded with eager and excited spectators, while the strife wages in the dusty arena below. Sweet perfume drops through the canopy which shelters from the burning sun, and clouds of dust rise from the chariot-wheels, from the glowing hoofs of the horses, and from the swift feet of those who run. By-and-by I hear a mighty shout that almost rends the welkin, as the plaudits of the thousands echo round the scene; and presently a man steps forward who has won the race, or slain the lion, or killed the gladiator, to receive from the Emperor's own hand a crown of laurel-leaves which fades by the very heat of the head that wears it. I notice also that the Emperor gives him a pure white stone, with his name written on it. He is now entitled, on presentation of that white stone ticket, to be fed at the country's expense, and to be fêted and honoured well nigh wheresoever he goes.

Now, the Christian life is a race; the Christian experience is a conflict. He who thinks by entering the church to escape the battle makes a great mistake. The battle wages wherever the name of Christ is spoken. Nor is it a strife which lasts a day, or a week, or a year.

> " 'Tis not the skirmish of an hour,
>   Sin yields not at a blow;
> For unbelief is hard to slay,
>   And that same foe you fight to-day
> Will be to-morrow's foe."

We must expect to fight if we enlist in the army of the Lord God of Hosts. We must not throw our harness off nor put our swords away.

> "Ne'er think the battle fought,
> Ne'er think the victory won,
> The work of faith will not be done
> Till we obtain the crown."

Some are called especially to endure hardness as good soldiers of Jesus Christ. It was so with the Pergamean Christians. Oh, what a dreadful place that they lived in! They were in the very forefront of the battle, and in the thick of the war. To be a soldier of Christ in the city of Pergamum was no sinecure; he could not be a carpet knight, but, like the men of Harlech, he was "foremost in the fray." We read of the city where this church existed, that it was the place where Satan dwelt, where Satan's seat was. Satan goeth to and fro in the earth seeking whom he may devour; he is always on the move, ever roaring upon his prey, but he has a seat, a court, a throne. There he holds high carnival, and thence he sends his myrmidons to do their fiendish business. Such a place was Pergamum, the head-quarters of the Skeleton Army, and the very throne of the arch-fiend himself. There it was that the altars of false gods were neither few nor far between; for in a single grove there were the shrines of Apollo, of Minerva, and of Jupiter, and, above all, of the celebrated Esculapius, the healing god, who was worshipped under the form of a serpent. Thus we find on some of the old Pergamean coins a figure of Esculapius with a rod in his hand, round which a snake is twining. So, literally, the throne of that old serpent, the devil, was there. You will not wonder, therefore, that they who dwelt at Pergamum and loved the Lord God of Israel had a hard time of it. There were temptations to idolatry on every hand. They could worship Jove if so disposed, or Minerva if her charms were greater; Apollo might attract them to his shrine; or if they chose they could demean themselves to worship Esculapius, and thereby prove themselves of their father, the devil. On every hand there were enchantments and allurements. But they did not yield. Firm to the faith, steadfast to the living and the true God, they remained, resolving to serve the God of their fathers, in spite of what others said or did. There were temptations to licentiousness of every sort, licentiousness all the more tempting because it was cloked with religiousness. Nor would they eat the food that had been offered to idols, for such a course was contrary to the mind and will of God. Against all these temptations, and the persecution which resistance to them involved, they continued steadfast, meriting the promise which Christ sent them, "To him that overcometh will I give to eat of the hidden manna."

It is not hard to believe that persecution arose in this place. They who resisted temptation were despised and rejected of men, and one believer, named Antipas, became a faithful martyr and witness; for he would not deny the faith, and was slain amongst them where Satan dwelt. Tradition tells us that this same Antipas was put within a red-hot brazen bull and burned to death; but when his tormentors expected to hear his shrieks and dying cries, they heard, proceeding from the mouth of the brazen bull, the prayers and praises of the faithful one, as his spirit soared away to meet his God. In these days of ours, thank God, we have not so much of open sin and idolatry to contend with, certainly not so much of fiery persecution to affright us, and yet it is true of many a Christian that he dwells where Satan's seat is. O God, it is a joy to us to be assured that thou knowest where we dwell, aye, and that thou dwellest with us too, for thou art a very present help in every time of trouble! If you, dear brother, are called upon to dwell in a very Sodom, the filthy communications of whose inhabitants vex you all the day and every day, be sure that the Lord knows where

A White Stone. 77

you are. "The Lord knoweth them that are his," and even in Sardis he has "a few who have not defiled their garments, and they shall walk with him in white, for they are worthy." Fight on; fight on; ne'er give the battle up. "In thy name we will set up our banners." Yes, dear Saviour, thou hast struggled, and fought, and conquered on our behalf, and we will conquer through thee too! I pray you to rise to the battle now. Grasp the sword once more; let your hands cleave unto the handle; buckle on the harness more firmly than ever, and determine that you will, through God's good grace, go on

> "From victory unto victory,
> Till every foe is vanquished,
> And Christ is Lord indeed."

Victory! victory! through the blood of the Lamb. Victory, through him that loved us!

And for what reward? "Be thou faithful unto death, and I will give thee a crown of life:"—no fading laurel, no myrtle branch which will soon decay, but an amaranthine coronet which on thy head shall sit so long as thou shalt live, or at least until thou takest it from off thy brow, to put it on the head of Jesus Christ thy Lord. Thank God for victory;—victory promised;—victory secured to all who fight for Jesus and in his strength.

> "As surely as he overcame,
> And triumph'd once for you;
> So surely you that love his name
> Shall triumph in him too."

II. PURITY. The scene is changed. I see now an ancient tribunal where the judges sit. There are lictors bearing the *fasces*, a bundle of sticks with an axe-head bound up amongst them, the symbol of justice and of punishment. I see the jurors in their places; I listen to the progress of the trial; and when all the witnesses have been heard, and the prisoner has made his own defence, I notice that into the ballot-box are cast some little stones. Some of them are white, others of them are black; but, thank God, the white stones predominate, and the foreman of the jury having counted them, declares that the prisoner is not guilty and should be dismissed; but in token of his innocence the judge delivers to him the pure white stone which tells him that he is not condemned. So in this place of sin, with all the enticements of evil, there were some who retained their purity and spotlessness—some who, like Joseph, fled at the tempter's voice—some who, like Daniel, could not forget the Lord their God—some who, like the holy children, would rather blaze in the furnace than bow before the image. To such the token of innocence was given. How is it with thee, my Christian friend? Hast thou kept thy garment unspotted from the world? In the world thou art and must be, of the world thou art not and must not be. How is it with thee? Examine yourselves, if ye be in the faith, and if there is the answer of a good conscience toward God which tells you that with all your faults you love him still, it shall be to you as the stone which releases you from all suspicion of guilt, and proclaims to men and angels that the Judge of all the earth himself has said, "Thou art all fair, there is no spot in thee." Is it not very appropriate that acquittal should be spoken of as a white stone? It becomes thenceforth a passport into bliss, for white is the livery of heaven. "And there shall in no wise enter into it anything that defileth." Those pearly portals refuse to turn upon their hinges to admit any but those whose garments are unspotted from the world. None but the blood-washed find entrance there.

> "Those holy gates for ever bar
> Pollution, sin, and shame;
> None can expect to enter there
> But followers of the Lamb."

O God, give to us this pure white stone, which shall tell us of our absolution through the blood of the Lamb. Holy and righteous and pure we are not, nor can be in and of ourselves, but if thou wilt speak us pardon, if thou wilt tell us that we are all fair and there is no spot in us, then we must, we will believe thee, for thy blood and it alone can wash us white as snow! Make this your prayer, as I make it mine, "Create in me a clean heart, O God, and renew a right spirit within me;" for this we know, that we shall never have the pure white stone unless we have the re-created, the snow-white heart.

Thus, then, we have spoken of victory and of purity.

III. NOVELTY. The manna is a new kind of food, far preferable to the meat offered to idols. "I will give him to eat of the hidden manna." The name is an entirely new name. Everything connected with our glorious religion is full of sparkling novelties. I remember to have seen one of Doré's celebrated pictures, entitled "The Entry of Christ into Jerusalem," shortly after it was painted, when the colours were all bright and beautiful, and though I much admired the drawing, I was particularly struck with the colouring. Everything seemed so fresh and new; of course it was in a new frame, and the very faces of the people seemed lighted up with a new joy as they beheld their King. The palm branches that the children waved seemed to be fresh grown and newly gathered. The very ground on which the happy people trod seemed bright with new-born sunshine, while the whole scene was a bright and beautiful representation of one of the most pleasing incidents in the life of our Lord. It is possible that the colours have faded before this, but this I know—that Christ's triumphal entry into the sinner's heart brings glorious sunshine, new joys, new hopes, new songs, new desires, new everything; for "Behold, I make all things new." We become "new creatures in Christ Jesus." We find that our names are included in the new covenant; the New Testament becomes to us the best and the brightest of all the books. We have a new heart to keep Christ's new commandments. We have a new life to carry us over our new troubles. We have new songs in our mouths, while we travel to the new Jerusalem by the new and living way, that is to say, his flesh, to find new joys and pleasures throughout eternity. Oh, it is a blessed thing to be a Christian, and those who think it is the same thing over and over again, on each Sunday and at every prayer-meeting, are mightily mistaken. Our experience is full of novelty, full of fresh joys, bright, beautiful, and refreshing.

The new name is the name of adoption. Adopted into another family, my new father's name becomes mine. By nature I am a child of wrath, even as others; by grace I am a child of God, an inheritor of the kingdom of heaven, for he has given us "the spirit of adoption, whereby we cry, Abba, Father." "Behold, what manner of love the Father hath bestowed upon us, that we should be called the sons of God."

Then there is the new name of espousal, for we are married unto him and he to us. Has he not said to us, "Thou shalt be no more termed Forsaken, neither shall thy land any more be termed Desolate, but thou shalt be called Hephzibah, that is, my delight is in her, and thy land Beulah, that is, married, for the Lord delighteth in thee, and thy land shall be married"? Oh, how sweet to lose our own old name, which was never worth the having, and as we embrace our husband to find his name attached to us—he the Christ and we the Christian.

There is the new name, too, of promotion for those who overcome. It were a grand thing to be a private in Christ's army, to belong to the rank and file of the Lord's elect; but when he says to us, "Come up higher, and I will exalt thee, for thou hast exalted me," it is better still, and this he does so often as we fight his battles well, and every victory leads to some fresh reward. You know the old story, I suppose, of how Napoleon at some grand review lost command over his restive steed, which straightway sped away, swift as an arrow from a bow, and how some private from the ranks, forgetting his place and duty, rushed from his position and seized the reins of the Imperial charger, and saved the royal life. Thereupon the Emperor turned round to him, and, cordially acknowledging his act of heroism, said, "Thank you, Captain." The soldier, believing all his master said, went never back into the ranks again, but claimed his right to be a Captain of the regiment. The story is generally told as exemplifying implicit confidence and faith, believing what God the Lord has spoken. But I have told it to illustrate the blessedness of promotion; for if you do doughty deeds for Jesus, not hanging back in the day of battle, be sure of this, you shall receive promotion instantly and certainly, and God himself will say, as it were, "Thank you, Captain," and you shall be at least one rank higher, not in your own esteem, but in God's, as the King delights to do his soldiers honour.

The new name that we shall get at last is the name of glorification. We may call ourselves what we like here, but after all we are not very much at the most—worms of the dust, and creatures of a day.

> "I'm but a stranger here,
> Heaven is my home."

Guilty sinners are we at the best, but oh, what a change when the glory-land dawns on our view! Worms now, we shall be angels them; sinful creatures at present, sons of the living God, and brighter than the seraphs shall we then appear. Here our songs are poor and paltry, there they will be full of fervour and harmony; here we were but pilgrims, as all our fathers were, there we shall be citizens of no mean city, for we shall have reached a city that hath foundations, whose builder and maker is God. Oh, let us thank God for the novelty which is always springing up about our Christian religion. Why, even as to temporal things we have new mercies fresh every morning, new blessings again at night, and the soul receives in its capacity new favours with each new sunbeam.

> " New mercies each returning day
> Hover around us while we pray,
> New perils past, new sins forgiven,
> New thoughts of God, new hopes of heaven."

IV. The next point is SECRECY. Just as the manna was hidden in the ark, so this hidden manna of which the Saviour speaks is laid up by God for those that love him.

The name he gives is unknown, except to those who receive it. The Christian religion, even to those who understand and love it, has much of mystery about it. It is the mystery of godliness. We cannot tell whence the wind bloweth, nor whither it goeth; so is every one that is born of God. There is a deal which cannot be revealed or proclaimed on the housetop; much that is meant to be hidden. Our holy faith is a thing of the inside, and the water that Christ gives us is a well of water within us, springing up unto everlasting life. What wonder, then, that to the world there is so much of mystery about us and our religion. The world cannot understand us, or our joys, or our sorrows. These are spiritual things, and must be spiritually discerned. We have a peace which is deep, far down beneath the surface, with which none can intermeddle. We have a joy which the world can no more take away from us than it can provide it for us, and an assurance of the Love of God within which only he that feels it knows. Well may we bless God, for the witness of the Spirit, for the earnest of the joy that is yet to be revealed, and that even now we have this happy token of all that is yet to fall to our glad lot. "The Lord knoweth them that are his," and

> "If one should ask of me how can I tell,
> Glory to Jesus, I know very well;
> God's Holy Spirit with mine doth agree,
> Constantly witnessing Jesus loves me."

V. Lastly, we speak of CHARITY. "To him that overcometh will I *give* to eat of the hidden manna, and will *give* him a pure white stone." Everything that we have is God's good gift. What hast thou that thou didst not receive? What of good hast thou evolved from thyself or created for thyself? Let us gladly own that all we have has come from above.

> "And every virtue we possess,
> And every victory won,
> And every thought of holiness,
> Are his alone."

Our temporal blessings are God's gracious gifts. The sun that shines upon us, that paints our flowers, and brightens our eyes, seems to say, "You do not deserve me;" the Providence that spreads our table, the dew and rain which fall upon us, the friends and relationships which comfort us, all seem to say, if but our ears would hear their voice, "You do not deserve us; you do not deserve us." O God, if thou wert swift to mark iniquity who amongst us could stand, and if we had our deserts we should have been damned ere this! All we have is a token of God's charity; it is inscribed with grace and beautiful with love divine. If we eat of hidden manna it is because he gives us to eat thereof, and if we have the earnest of the Spirit it is because he gives us the pure white stone. Some commentators think that there is a reference here to a stone called the *tessera hospitalis*. Let me tell you of the ancient custom. A small white stone was divided between two friends; one of them writing his own name on his portion of stone, his acquaintance inscribing his name on the other half; they then exchanged the stones, and in so doing exchanged one another's names. Henceforth they were able to go to one another's houses to partake of each other's hospitality; indeed, the stone became to each a passport to all that each possessed, and it is thought that the reference may be translated thus: Christ Jesus—and who is such a friend as he?—Christ Jesus comes to me, longing that I may be his friend. He breaks with me the *tessera*, the white stone. I see his name inscribed upon the portion that he gives me, and it seems to tell me that he longs to befriend me; and straightway, overcome by such matchless love, I write my name upon the other portion of the stone, and give it back to him; and thus there is a commerce betwixt the two, an interchange of possessions and of persons, and henceforward I am able to say, "My beloved is mine, and I am his;" henceforth I have a right to all he has; and he, of course, has a right to all I have, for what have I that I did not receive? There is thus a mutual compact betwixt us.

> "He is mine and I am his;
> What can I want beside?"

My heart is open to him; heaven is open to me. I am his property and he my possession; he holds me in his mighty hand, and I retain my hold on him with such faith as he gives me.

All this is doubly true of the life above. Beloved, this is not our rest. Yonder we look for the full fruition which is laid up for the saints who are "kept by the mighty power of God." Victory is possible here; it is certain there. Purity, at least in some measure, must be acquired here, for without holiness no man shall see the Lord, but purity is positive and spotless there. Novelty is our delight on earth, but in heaven there will be fresh surprises as each hour comes round, new joys throughout eternity. The secrecy and personal privacy of our faith and joy secure them to us even here, but in heaven it will be quite impossible for anyone to intermeddle with our sacred pleasures; there neither moth nor rust doth corrupt, and thieves do not break through nor steal. And as for charity and hospitality, why, brethren, heaven is a house of mercy, and the fact that we shall remain there when we have reached it is yet another proof of God's sovereign grace and of his power to save. Glory be to his ever-blessed name. When we are cast upon the shores of eternal bliss, we shall have to say, as Jonah did when he was once again upon *terra firma*, "Salvation is of the Lord." The present and future blessings of the Christian can never be reckoned up; they are far beyond the capacity of our poor weights and measures. While still in the flesh, the very poor are gloriously rich; the sick and suffering rejoice in tribulations also; and these are but the faint dawnings of the happy day, where all shall be joy and blessedness and peace.

May you and I have as much of joy here as we can bear, and experience the fulness of joy and the pleasures which are at God's right hand for evermore.

> "We shall have a new name in that land,
> In that land, that sunny sunny land;
> When we meet the bright angelic band
> In that sunny land.
>
> "We shall have it in a pure white stone,
> And no one will know the name therein;
> Only unto him that hath 'tis known
> When we're free from sin.
>
> "We shall eat the hidden manna there,
> At the marriage supper of the Lamb;
> We shall never hunger any more
> Who have overcome."

The Lord bless the message of his truth to all. Amen.

HEARING AND HEARKENING.

"But they have not all obeyed the Gospel."—*Romans* x. 16.

THERE is scarcely a place in all the world more remarkable for conversions than this Tabernacle. We could point to almost every pew and say, "This and that man was born there." And, oh, if these aisles could speak, and the forms on which you sit could but be mouthed and voiced, how gladly would they tell us of souls that have been born for heaven while listening to the preaching of the Gospel as declared in this house of prayer! There are very many tokens of God's favour resting upon the preacher and the people who are connected with this place—tokens which are unrivalled throughout the Christian world, and for which you, my beloved friends, can never be too thankful to the God of all grace. You will pardon me, I am sure, for saying that when far removed from you I have often thought how great is the privilege of those who hear sermons which, whether preached or printed, have ever proved to be the chosen vessels of God, conveying his saving grace to every one that believeth. BUT—BUT—(alas!

that there should be any "but" in such a joyful story)—
"*But* they have not all obeyed the Gospel." "They did not all hearken to the glad tidings," as the Revised Version has it.

What a happy thing it would be if we could say of this vast assembly and of every reader of the Sermons, "They have not only heard the glad tidings, but they have all accepted it"! How the bells of heaven would ring! What a shout of joy would swell around the throne as the angels rejoiced over every returning prodigal and each believing saint! But it is not so. The sweet music sounds already in heaven, for thousands have been born for God, and the ranks of the redeemed are ever swelling. But while I listen to the ringing of those happy bells, there seems to echo in my ears the solemn tolling of what will be a funeral bell to some unless they turn from the error of their ways; and the language of its iron tongue is, "But they have not all believed the Gospel. Not all! Not all! Not all!"

To such as have heard, but have not hearkened; to those who have come to the granary-door, but have never tasted that the Lord is good, I speak in the hope that a fresh voice and a different style may have the effect, through God's power, of inducing them to taste and see that the Lord is good.

I will remind you, first, that *you have all heard the glad tidings*. Secondly, I will endeavour to *show you the difference between hearing and obeying, or "hearkening."* And, thirdly, with God's help, I will *urge you to obey the Gospel*.

I. First, then, let me remind you that YOU HAVE ALL HEARD. The Apostle Paul is writing to the Romans, who, as you know, were Gentiles. He begins the chapter by speaking of Israel, the nation of promise, and declares that his prayer to God for Israel is that they might be saved. But Paul was particularly the Apostle to the Gentiles. To them was the Gospel sent by this notable servant of the Lord Jesus Christ, and it was his joy to traverse the most of the then known world, proclaiming wheresoever he went the glad tidings of salvation through a crucified Saviour. It is interesting to turn to the map on which are depicted the journeyings of the Apostle Paul,—to notice the red lines that cross the sea and traverse the countries, and to see the little crosses which mark the Apostle's stopping-places. Where'er he went he left the blood-red track behind him, for he proclaimed redemption through the blood of the Lamb, and where'er he tarried he lifted the Cross, for he was "determined not to know anything among men save Jesus Christ and him crucified." To some degree, even in the days of Paul, it could be said, "Have they not heard? Yes, verily, their sound is gone out into all the earth." Mars Hill had echoed with the story of the Cross, and the Roman palace was soon to hear of Jesus and his dying love, while almost everywhere the Saviour, of whom old Simeon had said that he was "a light to lighten the Gentiles," as well as "the glory of his people Israel," had been proclaimed in the hearing of all the people.

But if this was true of Paul's time, how trebly true is it to-day! These are the days, my brethren, in which knowledge is increased in the earth, and many run to and fro. The heathen idols bow themselves, as Dagon did before the ark of the covenant; and Buddha shall yet become as Baal, and all the false gods, and the false prophets too, shall hide their diminished heads, and the Crescent wane before the Cross. There is a printed Bible now for every man, and the

Cross is lifted far and wide, so that all who will may see. China's millions already hear of the Saviour who is to bring many sons of glory, and India's teeming multitudes listen to a Gospel which, received, will make them truly rich, and to the tribes of the Dark Continent a light has sprung up. The Maories of New Zealand have heard of a Saviour's love, and many of them have rejoiced in it believingly. Throughout the world the Gospel is winning its widening way, and on the wings of mighty love it flies, scattering its treasures in its flight. God is not unmindful of his covenant, for he is continuously rewarding Jesus for the travail of his soul, according to the promise that the uttermost parts of the earth shall be his possession, and the isles be glad because of him.

> "Fly abroad, thou mighty Gospel!
> Win and conquer; never cease.
> May thy lasting, wide dominions
> Multiply and still increase.
> Sway thy sceptre,
> Saviour, all the world around."

But apart altogether from the condition of the heathen world, the fact remains that all of *you* have heard the Gospel. People are very fond of arguing about the heathen. "What is to become of them"—they say—"who never heard of a Saviour's love and of the cross of Calvary?" The best way to answer such is to ask them the question, "What is going to become of you, for *you have heard?* You talk about those who sit in darkness, to whom, as yet, no light has sprung up. I talk to one who, though he sits in darkness still, cannot plead that no day star has arisen. You have seen that star quite plainly, and at times have been inclined to follow its bright beckonings, but you have remained disobedient to the heavenly vision." You remember, doubtless, the touching story of the dying gipsy boy who, being visited by a lady who told him of Jesus, the Saviour of sinners, poured this doleful lament into the missionary's ears, "Nobody ever told me! Nobody ever told me!" He died, muttering words which to his mother were altogether unintelligible, but which the good lady understood; for, as his spirit passed away, he shook his head and wept bitter tears, saying, "Nobody ever told me!" My friends, you cannot make that excuse before the throne of God, for you have all heard the Gospel, and, thousands of times, you have seen the plan of salvation plainly sketched before you. You have had it in your hands as the wayfarer holds the map; but you have wilfully and woefully taken the wrong track, preferring the broad road to the narrow way. Your sin "lieth at the door," and the crimson is on your own skirt.

We have in this chapter a very plain message concerning the way of salvation; and, lest you should say that the Gospel has not been preached to you, I should like to refer you to it. Look, for instance, at the 4th verse, which contains the very marrow of the Gospel. "For Christ is the end of the law for righteousness unto every one that believeth." Now, what is the end of the law? I take it that the end or object of the law is to bring life; "for Moses describeth the righteousness which is of the law in this wise, that he that doeth the works of the law shall live thereby." If, therefore, I keep the law *in toto*, I have a right to expect that I shall live by so doing. If I am sinless, I shall be without punishment. If I am pure and holy, I cannot come beneath the ban and judgment of a just and withal gracious God. How, then, is it that we do not live by the law? Not through any fault of the law, but through our own fault in that we have not kept it—in that, moreover, we have rendered ourselves incapable of keeping it. He that is guilty of breaking the law in one part or portion is guilty of the whole, so we must needs stand before God with heads bowed down, and hearts that bleed as we cry, "Unclean! Unclean!" "There is none that doeth good, no not one." But Christ is the end of the law. My righteousness is a thing impossible. Weave a spotless robe I cannot, but

> "Christ has done it, done it all,
> Long, long ago."

And, like his own vesture, this robe of righteousness which he gives to me is woven from the top throughout and covers me completely.

> "And lest the shadow of a spot
> Should on my soul be found,
> He takes the robe the Saviour wrought
> And casts it all around."

Receiving Christ as our substitute, and rejoicing in his righteousness imputed to us, we are accepted in the Beloved:—

> "With our Saviour's garments on,
> Holy as the Holy One."

So Christ is the end of the law to every one that believeth. He brings the life which the law would bring if we could but keep it, as he himself declares, "I am the way, the truth, and *the life*."

The "end of the law" refers also to the bearing of the dread penalty which the breakage of the law involves. A broken law cries loud to God for justice, and demands that he who broke it shall be punished; and the end of the law to the sinner can be only retribution. But Christ Jesus becomes to me the end of the law in that he bears my punishment. O blessed Christ, Emmanuel, thy wounds bespeak our peace! Thy cross is the pledge of our crown! We live because thou hast died!

> "By his death he brings me life;
> Peace is mine—he ends the strife;
> I am free—he paid the price.
> Glory to his name!"

This is the Gospel that you have heard over and over again.

Turn to the 9th verse: "If thou shalt confess with thy mouth the Lord Jesus, and shalt believe in thy heart that God raised him from the dead, thou shalt be saved." "Confess with thy mouth"! But you cannot do that until you believe in your heart. True, it is put first here, but we cannot confess what we do not possess. Believe in the Lord Jesus Christ with your heart, and then you cannot help confessing him with your mouth. Out of the abundance of the heart the mouth will speak. When you have within you the well-spring of love to Jesus, you will say, "We love him because he first loved us;" and you will know that you are assuredly saved, not through confession, but through faith in the ever-blessed Son of God.

Let me commend the 13th verse to the notice of every seeking sinner: "Whosoever shall call upon the name of the Lord shall be saved." What is it to call on the name of the Lord? "To pray," says one. Well; but what is it to pray? Not to say prayers—not merely to utter a wish, or to express a sentiment. To "call upon the name of the

Lord," I take it, is nothing less than to believe in the work and to rely upon the merits of the Redeemer; for "How shall they call on him on whom they have not believed?" I warrant you do not summon a physician in whom you do not believe, nor will you call on Christ, the Great Physician, unless you are persuaded that he is both able and willing to cope with your disease and to meet your desperate case. That word "whosoever" is one of the sweetest words in all God's book, for it sets the door so widely open and admits every one to the presence of the King. All the barriers are taken away when "Whosoever" is the porter at the gate. There is a way by which the worst can come to God, the "whosoever" way, for Jesus Christ, the Lord over all, is rich unto all that call upon him, whether they be Greek or Jew, barbarian, Scythian, bond or free.

We have heard of an eccentric individual who, having made a large hole in a gateway for his great St. Bernard dog, cut a small one for his little terrier's use. It struck most people that the opening that was large enough for the St. Bernard would readily have let the little fellow through. Do you not think so? So also it seems to me that this great door that Christ has set—the open door, of "Whosoever," which let Manasseh, and Saul of Tarsus, and the dying thief, and the adulterous woman, and a host of other sinners into the kingdom—will do for me: not that I am a less sinner than they, but, being as great as they, I do not wish a larger door. Moreover, if it could be necessary I should not ask in vain, for this "Whosoever" door seems to be made of elastic, and stretches as widely open as the sinner needs; at all events, there is no bolt across, and nothing to prevent boldness of access. By the new and living way the vilest sinner may find grace to help in every time of need.

Hearing and Hearkening.

II. Let me try to show you THE DIFFERENCE BETWEEN HEARING AND OBEYING. The fact that the Apostle laments that they did not all obey, implies that some did. Wherever the Gospel is preached some will receive the truth in the love of it and bind it to their hearts. We would not cease to preach the Gospel even if encouraging results did not follow; but we are the more ready to labour on when we are assured that our labour is not in vain in the Lord. Some one asked if the people of New Zealand would listen to the Gospel. Did he think that we wanted a different sort of Gospel for the ends of the earth—an article specially manufactured for the Colonies? My experience is that wherever the old truths are clearly and earnestly preached, there are ears to hear them and hearts to understand. Until a better Gospel is given to us, which can never be, our intention is to go on preaching the atonement and substitution of our Lord Jesus Christ, persuaded that God's word shall not return unto him void, but that it shall accomplish his purpose, and prosper in the thing whereto he sent it forth.

But, alas, I must confess that in New Zealand, as well as in Old England, there are many who, though they hear it, do not hearken to it. I will try to show you the difference. We have in the Colonies a custom in connection with the Fire Brigade which will illustrate my point. The city is divided into numbered wards, and when the alarm has been sounded, the bell tolls out the number of the ward in which the conflagration has occurred. By this arrangement those who are from home, attending a service or visiting their friends, are informed of the locality of the fire. Suppose the system could be amplified, so that every street and each house were indicated; what eager listening there would be! When the bell had finished clanging its alarm, would not every householder count the strokes? and he who heard the number of his house sounded out, would have wings to his heels immediately, and rush away to save his children and his goods from the fiery element. Now, it is when the Gospel comes home to a man like that,—when he hears his number rung out, and feels that his soul is in danger of eternal burning,—when the finger of God points at him as Nathan's did at David, and a stern voice declares "Thou art the man"—then it is that he has given up hearing for hearkening, and hearkening becomes equivalent to obeying. Then he hastens to the Saviour, saying, "I flee unto thee to hide me." Oh that many of my hearers and readers would understand that the Gospel comes to them,— that they already tremble on the brink of eternal ruin, and that the Saviour's arms are stretched out on purpose to save *them.* Then would they accept—then would they hearken —then would they obey. God grant that it may be so.

Perhaps another illustration will make this clearer still. There is a large crowd in the street, and I hear the bellman's ringing, and his stentorian voice crying out, "Oh yes, oh yes, oh yes." He proceeds to announce that as the inhabitants of the town are perishing for lack of bread, and shivering for want of clothing, certain friends have opened a soup kitchen yonder, and others in another place are giving blankets and clothes away. The starving, shivering people listen with all-eager interest. Oh, what glad tidings it is to them—bread enough and to spare, and soup into the bargain, and blankets too. "Oh," they say; "this is just the thing for us." No, they do not stop to say that. Away they go, without comment, to receive the bounty. They listen first, and then they hearken. They no sooner hear

Hearing and Hearkening.

than they obey. But, while the crowd was listening to the bellman, a fine lady in a grand carriage said to the coachman, "John, what is the matter there? Just pull up a minute. I would like to see what is wrong." Thereupon the splendid equipage neared the crowd, but did not remain, for her ladyship was disgusted as soon as she saw so many poor, hungry, ill-clothed folk, and said, peevishly, "Drive on, John; drive home." She did not want any soup and blankets, not she. She could readily have spared half of hers for the poor and needy, so of course she does not obey the bellman. I am persuaded that the great reason why there are so few hearkeners among so many hearers of the glad tidings is that they do not realize their necessities. "We are rich and increased in goods. We have need of nothing," say they, and away they roll in the chariot of self-righteousness; whereas the poor, starving, shivering sinners say, "This is glad tidings indeed. Ring that bell again; tell us the good news once more;" and away they hie to Jesus. And what does he give them? Bread—the best they ever ate—better than angels' food, for

> "Never did angels taste above
> Redeeming grace and dying love."

And he gives them the wine of his own pomegranates to wash the bread down with. To this he adds the silken clothing of his own righteousness and favour. He gives them money, too—the gold of the kingdom—and makes them rich to all eternity. They hearken to and obey the Gospel.

Since the glad tidings have rung so often in your ears, you should obey at once. You must believe on your own account in the Lord Jesus Christ. It must be a personal matter. God himself cannot do it for you, the preacher cannot accomplish it on your behalf, nor can those who pray for you. Once upon a time the prophet Elisha went up from Jericho with the sons of the prophets to build a house —the first pastors' college. Over Jordan they passed, each man armed with an axe, and having reached the forest they set to work to cut down the trees. While they were thus engaged—for accidents will happen even in so well regulated a family, occupied, too, in work for God—an axe-head slipped off its handle and fell into the water. "Alas, master," said the young prophet, "Alas, master, for it was borrowed." "Show me the place," replied his master. "Where did it fall in?" "Just *there*," said the young man. "I wish you could get it back again, for it is not mine. The loss would be serious enough if it were; but it is worse since it belongs to So-and-so." Then the prophet cut down a stick from a neighbouring tree, and having thrown it into the water, "the iron did swim." God wrought a miracle. That floating axe-head was the first ironclad ever made. Towards the prophet it swam, and grounded on the edge of the bank. Then said the man of God to the young man, who I suppose was looking and wondering, "Take it up to thee," and doubtless the tone of his voice implied, "Do not stand looking. Put it on the handle once more, and make up for lost time, and fell that tree. Take it up to thee." When God works a miracle, he does not destroy the necessity for effort and exertion on our part. In the matter of your soul's salvation, God will make the iron swim. None but he can change your heart. He has already cast the "wondrous cross" into the stream, and provided a perfect salvation. Pardon lies at your feet. "Take it up to thee." Salvation is already wrought, completely made; the atonement needs no addition, but you must grasp it : you must make it yours. Oh, I pray you, accept Christ's salvation at once. It is the free gift of God; and since so many years have already been lost, set to work for God, bringing down the tall trees, labouring for Jesus with an energy which seems determined, if possible, to make amends for wasted hours and misspent years, and all the sins that have been crowded into them.

III. Now, lastly, LET ME URGE YOU TO OBEY. You have heard the tidings. You cannot doubt that it is *glad* tidings, for it tells of escape from hell and entrance into heaven. Some of you have been pleaded with to accept the Gospel— pleaded with by loving mothers, and anxious fathers, and faithful pastors ; and you have seen others accepting Christ, and believing the good tidings. Oh, if your friends have already decided for Christ, imitate their good example. They are rejoicing in a new friend. Show your friendship with them by making friends with Jesus. Moreover, you have been *impressed* with the glad tidings, if I mistake not, but you have gone away like the man who saw his natural face in the glass, but straightway forgot what manner of man he was. Many there are who have been determined to fear God and to trust Christ for years, and they have not done it yet. "To-morrow," they say, "to-morrow, to-morrow." "To-morrow" is their favourite day. And yet "to-morrow" never comes.

"I will to-morrow, that I will, I will be sure to do it;
To-morrow comes, to-morrow goes, and still thou art to do it.
Thus, then, repentance is delayed from one day to another,
Until the day of death is one, and judgment is the other."

Procrastinate no longer. Accept the joyful tidings and the Saviour of whom the tidings speak.

Why do so many remain disobedient to this heavenly vision? Either they do not realize their need, or else they do not recognize the richness of the supply. It must be one or the other.

Stretch yourselves in imagination on a couch. You are lying half asleep in a room on the wall of which is a simple picture. At a cottage door a poor wayfarer sits upon a fallen log. He looks hungry and tired; and just in the porchway there stands a kind-looking country woman with a baby in her arms, and a little child beside her with a basin of porridge or of soup in its hands. The little one is being taught by its mother to be good and kind to the poor. Now close your eyes again and go to sleep and think over the picture. You will wake up presently and look at the view again. Has anything happened? Oh no, the beggar still sits at the door and looks as hungry as ever; the child still holds out the porridge, and the mother still looks on. You wonder why the wanderer does not take the soup, for he seems to need it, and there is a kind expression on the mother's face, and the child seems glad to play the part of "Charity." How is it that want and weariness do not eagerly accept kindness and refreshment? The answer is found in the fact that it is not real life at all; it is only a picture. The man has no real needs, he is not actually hungry, nor is it a basin of porridge at all, and the smile on the woman's face is only pictured. There is nothing real in all of it, or the dinner would soon be demolished, the famished fed, and the giver gratified. There are some who do not accept the offered mercy because its glorious reality has never dawned upon them; nor are they aware of the reality of their need, though they may have a dreamy sense of the fact that something is wanting. The loving smile upon Christ's face, and the richness of his mercy, seem uncertain to them, or are judged "too good to be true." So they go hungry and thirsty and tired still, and mercy's arms are still outstretched, and peace and pardon offered.

The closing verses of this chapter are some of the sweetest in God's word. "All the day long have I stretched out my hands to a disobedient and gainsaying people." Oh the mercy of God! The mercy of God! It is enough to break us down into contrition to think that he has stretched out his hands all day long. Did you ever try to hold up your hand at arm's-length for half an hour? I warrant you you will soon get tired of it. The blood will all run from your fingers' ends, and out of your arm, and you will soon be weary. Even Moses needed two strong helpers to hold up his arms. But God says, "*All day long I have stretched forth my hands.*" Nor has he yet grown tired—blessed be his holy name. Still he holds out the hands of entreaty.

"There for me my Saviour stands,
  Shows his wounds and spreads his hands."

All day long—in early infancy, buoyant youthhood, middle age, old age—still he holds them out. You know how the ancient orators used to address the multitude. Raphael depicts Paul preaching at Athens with his hands outstretched exhorting the people. And so Demosthenes, and Peter the Hermit, and all who have stirred the masses, emphasized their matter by appropriate manner. The outstretched hands spoke of earnest longing and urgent entreaty. Just so God in Jesus has been pleading, and entreating, and exhorting with outstretched hands all your life long, that you should be reconciled to him and trust in Christ.

But this imagery may refer to a mother who is teaching her little one to walk. You know how she manages it. There stands a little toddling child. The mother draws back inch by inch, perhaps on her knees, and, with her arms held out lovingly, tells her little one to run into them. So the Lord encourages the trembling sinner whose faith is very tottering. Does he not seem to say, "How can I give thee up? O Ephraim, how can I give thee up? Run into my arms. Be reconciled to me." Thus the trembling footsteps of the new-born faith are helped to totter towards the Saviour. "Return, return, ye wanderers: return." O Father God, into the open arms of thy dear Son we run. Thou hast stretched them out in vain too long already, yet not too long, for if thou hadst not stretched them out so long many of us would have been damned ere this. We are sinful indeed, in that we have kept thee waiting all these years, but "it is better late than never."

> "Though guilty, weak, and helpless worms,
>   On thy kind arms we fall:
> Be thou our strength, our righteousness,
>   Our Saviour and our all."

I pray you give not sleep to your eyes, nor slumber to your eyelids, until you also have obeyed the Gospel and hearkened to the glad tidings. The Lord help you so to do. Amen.

A FAIR WIND.*

"And after one day the south wind blew."—*Acts* xxviii. 13.

THE whole verse reads, "And from Syracuse we fetched a compass, and came to Rhegium; and after one day the south wind blew, and we came the next day to Puteoli." I expect that most of you are sufficiently well acquainted with the geography of the part of the world referred to in our text to render it unnecessary for me to give you any very particular details. However, the more vividly the position is before your minds, the more interesting will our meditation prove. To put it very simply, if not exactly, we will say that Syracuse is the most southerly town of the three, and that the others are in a line above it northwards—Syracuse, Rhegium, Puteoli. Syracuse, as you know, is in the south of Sicily; Rhegium, in Italy, near the toe of the boot; and Puteoli a little farther north than the lovely Bay of Naples. A while ago it was my pleasurable lot to steer much the same course; but travelling nowadays is very different from what it was in the days of Paul. We were not obliged to tack through the Straits of Messina,

---

* Delivered in South Street Baptist Church, Greenwich—Pastor C. Spurgeon's.

nor were we wind-bound at Rhegium; but though we anchored for a while in the beautiful Bay of Neapolis rather than in that of Puteoli, there was sufficient to remind us of the troubles of the Apostle. The ship in which Paul sailed was an Alexandrian corn ship, called the Dioscuri, or the Twin Brothers, whose names were Castor and Pollux. They were the sons of Jupiter, supposed to rule the winds and waves. As far as Rhegium the ship had a comparatively prosperous voyage; but the cargo which was for that port having been discharged, the captain looked in vain for a favouring breeze. Either a calm prevailed at that time which prevented them getting out of the harbour, or else a north wind was blowing, which would be dead ahead. Anxiously did the skipper trace the sky for signs of an approaching breeze, or for indications that the rude north blast would change into a southerly zephyr. I do not know if the mariners in those days had learned to whistle for the wind. Perhaps they were so employed; but then, as now, whistling was waste of breath. The wind bloweth where it listeth, and whistles when it pleases, whether we whistle or no. By-and-by, in God's good providence, not because the captain wished it, nor because the sailors whistled for it, but because heaven's order had gone forth, the wind veered round to the south, or else the calm became disturbed by a breeze, which seemed to be made on purpose for the north-bound craft. You may be sure that all was bustle immediately; up came the anchor, up went the sails, and away the galley flew before the favouring breeze. The passage was a quick one, too, for they came the next day to Puteoli.

But it is my purpose to speak not so much of ships and sailors, as of Christians and of their trials. Many of the Lord's people find themselves in just the difficulty that the

"Castor and Pollux" experienced at Rhegium. They are wind-bound. Like the patriarch, they cry, "All things are against me." The strong current setting through the Straits of Messina, and the contrary wind, are types of the hindrances and obstacles which assail the heaven-bound voyager.

Have we not often found the tide running against us, and the wind right ahead, till in the bitterness of distress we have said, "O God, why are we thus? It seems as if thy providence had grown unkind, and thou thyself forgetful of thine own. How is it that we who love thee, and strive to serve thee, are thus hampered, and hindered, and prevented, even in our work for thee?" There is much to help us in this subject, and if he who holds the winds in his fist will be so gracious as to let the south wind out, the sweet zephyrs of encouragement will waft us on to better prospects, and to stronger faith.

Three simple facts attract our notice. Firstly, *The wind was for a while unfavourable;* secondly, *It soon became fair;* and thirdly, *The opportunity was immediately seized.*

I. THE WIND WAS AT FIRST UNFAVOURABLE. I do not see what right we have, as men and women, much less as Christian men and women, to expect everything to favour us.

My dear brother, remember that *thou art a man,* and that man is born to trouble as the sparks fly upward. Thou art a frail, weak creature, fearfully and wonderfully made, but the more liable, in consequence of the delicacy of thy body's mechanism, to be a prey to disease and death. Do not wonder that things go wrong with thee sometimes. When thou hast shuffled off this mortal coil, and canst soar through worlds unknown, disease will not reach thee: dyspepsia and indigestion, and all the ills that flesh is heir to, will be things of the past. That which is born of the flesh is flesh, and consequently frail.

But, further, *thou art a sinful man.* Sin is itself the greatest trouble, and the fruitful cause of every grief. We all have sinned and come short of the glory of God; and "shall a living man complain—a man for the punishment of his sins?" Since Adam and his wife forgot and disobeyed their God, the perspiration has stood upon the foreheads of their sons; while the greatest joy of their daughters has been accompanied with pain and sorrow. Sin has blighted this fair world of ours, and spread thorns and thistles where else all had been lilies and roses. We are sinful men, and consequently cannot expect but that the wind will be against us, and that trouble and disappointment and tribulation will meet us as punishments for our iniquities.

Perhaps, dear friend, you are *a seeker after Christ,* longing for peace and crying for pardon, and you say to yourself sometimes, "I am on a good errand, why should I find it so difficult? Why is the road so rough? At Christ's command I am seeking first the kingdom of God and his righteousness. Yet I do not succeed. Everything seems unfavourable. Conscience speaks against me: the devil roars upon me: God's people do not always favour and encourage me: sometimes God's word looks as black as midnight, and the preaching of the Gospel has no sounds of love and mercy for me." Why, dear friend, thou art wind-bound in the harbour of Rhegium, so to speak; but, believe me, the prize is so well worth having that you may be well content to seek it long and earnestly. It is no easy matter to be saved. In one sense it is simplicity itself —"Believe on the Lord Jesus Christ and thou shalt be saved"; but to believe is not mere child's play. All things are possible to him that believeth, but to believe is impossible to the unregenerate heart. Christ himself has said, "*Strive* to enter in at the strait gate," and again, "The kingdom of God suffereth violence, and the violent take it by force." Zaccheus had to climb up a tree and down again before Christ came into his house and brought salvation with him. The sick woman had to elbow her way through the crowd to get at the hem of Jesus' garment. The Syrophenician found she must plead and argue with her Lord before she got even the crumbs that fell from the Master's table. Let no seeker be surprised if history repeats itself in his or her case. "Ye shall seek me," saith the Lord, "and find me *when ye shall search for me with all your heart.*" Do not despair because of discouragement, but believe that the Lord is only drawing you to himself, and longs as much as you do that he and you should be reconciled.

But you are a *Christian man:* you have already trusted Christ and been baptized—at least I hope so—and joined the church. And did you fancy that when you became identified with the Lord's people you would be beyond the bounds of trouble?—

> "Safe from the world's temptations,
> Safe from corroding cares."

This is not true of the arms of the church, for though it is a fold, its hurdles can be leaped by the devouring lion, and Christ's disciples are sent forth "as sheep in the midst of wolves." The inventory of the Christian's possessions is not complete if "with persecutions" be omitted.

> "Must I be carried to the skies,
>   On flowery beds of ease,
> Whilst others fought to win the prize,
>   And sailed through bloody seas?
>
> Are there no storms for me to face?
>   Must I not stem the flood?
> Is this vile world a friend to grace
>   To help me on to God?"

Indeed it is not. Upon the lake of Galilee the servants of the Saviour, aye, and the Saviour himself, were "toiling in rowing, for the wind was contrary."

Do not expect, then, to have everything your own way. Do not hope that the wind will remain astern of you whichever way you like to turn the helm of your barque, or that it will alter its direction to suit your convenience. God has the ruling of the winds and waves, and if he should sometimes send adverse currents and contrary breezes, tarry in the harbour of resignation till the time is fulfilled and his will accomplished.

Note next that *a head-wind to us may be favourable to other people.* We are at times very selfish in our prayers. For instance—I pray the Lord for rain because my cabbages want it; but then my neighbour would prefer sunshine for his corn. I have every right to ask the Lord to bless my garden, I know, but I must not be surly if he prefers to bless my neighbour's field. My loss is somebody else's gain. Do you say that it is very hard to look at it that way? I know it is, but there is nothing impossible to the Christian, and it is the spirit of the Master after all. O Saviour, what a dreadful whirlwind was that which blew against thy barque and shattered it upon the hill of Calvary, and yet it was the best breeze that ever blew for sinners. The substitution of the Lord Jesus Christ is our example, and it is as you and I live and act and pray and think in that same spirit that we shall find that what works us ill is working good elsewhere, and that is, indirectly, good to us. "It is an ill wind that blows nobody any good." Perhaps there was a calm in this case, and God was making rain for future days, and by evaporation forming the clouds to shelter tender fruit from excessive sunshine. Perhaps the north wind was blowing. Well, that was just the thing for the vessels that were bound south, was it not? However would they have got on if the south wind had sprung up before they got to their desired haven? Oh to have that spirit always which will say, "Lord, if I had my choice I would have the south wind, for I want to go right away north; but then there is somebody who wants to come south, so, Lord, I leave the wind, as well I may, in thy hand. It shall be good for me though it does not seem so. The Lord will withhold no good thing from those that walk uprightly."

The winds are proverbially fickle. Who can manage them? *God can!* We speak of the laws by which the winds are governed, and science is constantly showing plainer proofs that there are such laws, but, mind you, they are not nature's laws, but those of nature's God. We who preach the Gospel simply, and think like this upon these scientific matters, are blamed for not going "deep enough." I have the impression that we go just a little deeper than the scientists, for they say that the winds are controlled by natural laws. Such a theory is as shallow as a milk-pan. I go deeper, and I say that these natural laws are controlled by God. I heard it said the other day, in the Metropolitan Tabernacle, that when God made the world, he did not wind it up like a watch, and then put it under his pillow and go to sleep. Not he, indeed. He made it, and then set it agoing, but he still directs its course, and regulates its forces, "upholding all things by the word of his power."

> "He rides upon the stormy wind,
> And manages the seas."

I am not sure that we do not talk sometimes rather irreverently, though unwittingly so, about the "clerk of the weather." I know no clerk of the weather except God. "He causeth his wind to blow and the waters flow." "He bringeth his wind out of his treasuries. He rode upon a cherub and did fly: yea he did fly upon the wings of the wind." Now, if the winds, more fickle than anything and everything besides, are governed and controlled by the Master-maker's hand, every coincidence so called, every circumstance, every *accident*, is just as much under the gracious influence of a faithful Creator. O thou who makest the clouds thy chariot—thou who alone canst say, awake, O north wind, or come thou south—thou who canst break the ships of Tarshish with an east wind, or waft the Alexandrian corn ship on her peaceful way to Puteoli,—I am sure that the storm, in the teeth of which I have to force my way, is as much the creation of thy providence as the soft breeze, laden with perfume, that sometimes wafts me toward my desired haven! It will soothe thy sorrows, troubled heart, if thou canst believe this for thyself. It will make thee happy in all circumstances, and thy contented mind shall be a continual feast. O what joy it is to leave everything in the hands of God, to let him cast the lot into the lap as well as to dispose of it. It is recorded of Napoleon Bonaparte that having spoken boastfully in the presence of friends about his projected invasion

A Fair Wind.

of Russia, and being rebuked by a good lady, who ventured to say, "Sire, man proposes, but God disposes," the haughty emperor replied, as angrily as he well could to a lady, "I dispose as well as propose." Thereupon he marched his millions into Russia, but never brought them back again; and all the snowy plains were incarnadined with Frenchmen's blood; while he himself tasted the bitterness of defeat, and already felt his throne tottering beneath him. 'Tis better far to

> "Leave to his soverign hand
> To will and to command."

How powerless we are to direct our own affairs! The ship of which we speak was named the "Castor and Pollux," and these two sons of Jove were supposed to have power over winds and waves. Why, then, did they not turn the wind round to suit their purpose? "Surely it is an easy matter for you, O sons of Jove, to make the breezes favourable! What means your name if you cannot help yourselves in this emergency? What's in a name indeed?" It is interesting to recall the names of some vessels that have been wrecked—"The Happy Return" never came back again; "The Success" was a terrible failure; and "The Prosperous" never paid a dividend. Just before I left the harbour of Auckland, I saw floating in the harbour, with a yawning gap in her bows, a steamer named "The Triumph." What a misnomer to be sure for a vessel that ran upon a rock right under the rays of a lighthouse, and was with the greatest difficulty floated again. So they call their ships, but the winds and the waves triumph over them, and play with them like toys. And so we name our schemes and resolutions, and dote upon them, forgetting that God can break our ships and bring our counsels to nought. Well is it for us that he does sometimes, yet we do not always think so. I like the spirit of the man who, having a large vane to tell which way the wind blew, cut in the zinc, "God is love." O to learn this lesson well! If the wind blows from the north, "God is love." If it blows from the south, "God is love." If it comes from the west, "God is love." Aye, and if we have that bitter cold east wind, that is good for neither man nor beast, "God is love" just the same. Is he not God of the whole earth and blessed for ever? My heart adores thee, mighty Maker! "The east and the west, thou hast created them. Tabor and Hermon shall rejoice in thy name," and I will rejoice too, whichever way the wind blows.

II. THE NORTH WIND PRESENTLY BECAME FAIR. "It is a long lane that has no turning." All things come to the man that can wait; and as to the Christian, why, it ought to be his pleasure to wait.

> "Wait thou his time; so shall the night
> Soon end in glorious day."

"I will trust and not be afraid." "Why art thou cast down, O my soul, and why art thou disquieted in me? Hope thou in God, for I shall yet praise him, who is the health of my countenance and my God." And was it not worth waiting for? When the breeze did spring up it was one of the best the skipper had ever experienced. It blew from exactly the right quarter, was neither too light nor too stiff, and, if I mistake not, the "Castor and Pollux" made the fastest passage on record from Rhegium to Puteoli, for it is recorded in the apostolic log-book, "We came the next day to Puteoli." The Lord was waiting to be gracious. God was brewing that south wind while the passengers and crew were vexing themselves about the north wind. And so while I am waiting and longing, and wishing, and perhaps fretting and grumbling, God is getting my blessing ready for me—waiting to be gracious. My soul, wait thou only upon God!

And this applies to the seekers of whom I spoke just now. You are crying, "Oh, that I knew where I might find him," and while you are yet speaking God is preparing a south wind. Do you not already feel its breath? Listen to this. It comes like a zephyr from the south—"Him that cometh to me I will in no wise cast out." Does not that blow your way, and fit your case, and swell your sails? Oh that you would spread the canvas and catch the breeze. Or try this: "I, even I, am he that blotteth out thy transgressions for mine own sake, and will not remember thy sins." Does not that suit you? "Let him that heareth say come. And let him that is athirst come. And whosoever will, let him take the water of life freely." These passages are as the breath of God, breezes from his heart of love, on which full many a mariner has relied, and they have carried them sweetly and safely to that happy region where

> "Not a wave of trouble rolls
> Across the peaceful breast."

III. AS SOON AS IT DID BECOME FAIR THE SAILORS SEIZED THE OPPORTUNITY. "Of course they did," say you. Well, I do not know why "of course," except that they were men of common sense. I would to God that all had common sense about spiritual things, and then I believe that all would "of course" be saved. Have you not heard many a sermon after which you have said "I cannot understand how any one could go away unconverted. How could they help trusting in the Lord Jesus after that invitation, and after so sweet and plain a proclamation of the way of life?" The only reason is that the mind is darkened and the heart is hardened by unbelief. There is no "of course" about till God makes his people willing in the day of his power. But see what these mariners did. Perhaps there was quite a flotilla of vessels in that port, and as soon as the wind changed the anchor chains began to click, and the sails to flap, but being once filled with the breeze, away sped each north-bound craft, through the harbour heads, while onlookers on the shore said one to another, "There go the ships! There go the ships!" Yes, there they go. Why should they not go? The wind said "Go," and they obeyed its voice. And we may do likewise in temporal and spiritual matters. 'Tis said that "There is a tide in the affairs of men which, taken at the flood, leads on to fortune." However this may be, I am convinced that many an opportunity is lost by people who, for want of confidence in themselves, or more often through want of trust in God, do not set sail till the breeze is gone. It is sadly so in spiritual matters. Repentance is too often delayed till death; and the foolish virgins come to the supper when the door is shut.

We will suppose that the harbour is full of little vessels, all bound north. The south wind springs up, but, strange to say, there is no movement in all the fleet. Each ship remains as still as if it were a painted ship upon a painted ocean. Whatever has happened? The wonder increases. There is one vessel's crew putting another anchor down and working hard at it too, for fear they should be wafted against their will towards what ought to be the desired haven. I saw a woodcut the other day of a vessel in full sail but with

A Fair Wind. 115

her anchor holding fast to the rocks beneath. Never was such an absurdity practised in seafaring life, but I know many people, who when the Gospel is preached and impressions are being made, instead of pulling the anchor up and yielding to God's good Spirit, run out yet another lest they should be converted. One man told me to my face that he did not come to chapel because he was afraid he should be converted. Afraid of being converted! Afraid of getting to heaven! Afraid of escaping hell! Afraid of Jesus and of God! I pray you act not thus.

There is another vessel on which the crew and the skipper are fast asleep. They "turned in" as soon as the south wind blew. These are they who are unconcerned about their salvation. They know that they are voyaging somewhere, but they care not whither. They know that there is a possibility for them to be saved as well as others, but they wrap themselves about with self-satisfaction, and live in the slumber-land of unconcern. They are asleep. No, they are dead—" Dead in trespasses and sins." O man, wake up, put up thy sails and work thy vessel, for God will never save thee else. There must be some desire on thy part as well as power on his part. Let the mill-wheel go round, for the water is flowing into its buckets. Let the flower open, for the sun is shining upon it. And do thou the same to the genial influences of God's good grace, and thou shalt be blessed in so doing.

There is another vessel on board of which the most peculiar performance possible is going on. Mark you, there is a splendid wind blowing—what the sailors call a "spanking breeze"; and yet these men are actually endeavouring to move their craft with artificial airs. One of them has a blow-pipe in his hands, and with which he tries to blow the vessel along. Another uses a pair of bellows for the same purpose. Several of them are waving fans, and seeking to waft their ship towards Puteoli. Fools that they are. God's breath is better than the little breeze they make. And who are these? These are the self-righteous, who say, "You tell us that there is a righteousness provided by God, but we are above taking that." They want to work out a righteousness of their own, and they are puffing and blowing, and trying to speed their barques towards heaven.

What supreme folly it is. God has done it : Christ has done it—

> "Done it all
> Long, long ago."

Fellow sinner, thou hast but to seize the helm, or, better still, hand it over to the captain of thy salvation. Keep a good look out forward by all means ; see to the trimming of the sails, of course ; work out your own salvation with fear and trembling, but remember that it is God who worketh in you to will and to do of his good pleasure. Be not amongst those who being ignorant of God's righteousness seek to establish a righteousness of their own, or like the sailors who, ignoring the south wind, seek to make breezes by their own endeavours.

There is yet another ship to notice. No one appears on the deck, for the sailors and officers are poring over maps, and parchments, and charts. One of them is the theory of storms. Another is a work on navigation. Another is a description of the currents, and the depth of the ocean. Another is a chart of quite another part of the world. But every one is deeply intent upon these works. They seem to have forgotten that there is a fair breeze blowing, and possibly do not mean to set sail till they have mastered their geometry and geography. Do you know who these people represent? These are they who say, "No, I want to understand everything fully before I believe anything at all. I must know how I am going to round the promontory of election, and how I can reconcile the current of God's sovereignty with the counter-current of man's responsibility! I cannot blame any one for wishing to comprehend the deep things of God, nor would I dissuade you from inquiring about predestination, but such inquiries must not prevent the use of the means of grace, or the acceptance of the truth as it is in Jesus. For the present it suffices me that God's mercy is for all and upon all them that believe. "Christ Jesus came into the world to save sinners." I am a sinner. Am I an elected sinner? Yes, if I trust in Christ. I therefore hearken to the Gospel, yield to its influences, and having started on the voyage believingly, I remain assured that he will bring me to the desired haven, and perfect that which concerneth me.

Notice, lastly, that they came ere long to Puteoli. There were wells at Puteoli, and palms and fountains, and doubtless weary travellers rejoiced in these. There, too, the Apostle "found brethren." Oh, if thou wilt come to Christ thou shalt find a well of living water, a bath of precious blood that washes white as snow, a fountain which will be in your heart like a well of water springing up unto everlasting life. And there are brethren too—the elder brother, God's dear Son, and all the children of the family, who will welcome you into the church and go with you hand-in-hand to glory.

But Paul did not stop at Puteoli. He had to go overland then to Rome; and, as you know, at Rome he laid down his life for Jesus' sake. But Rome was not the terminus of his journey. That is where the red line on the map stops, but we want a celestial map to show his real resting-place. No, I forgot; he has not stopped yet, for he is journeying on and on, ever making progression, ever getting nearer to the Saviour's face. And I believe that every Christian, though he be shipwrecked at Melita—though he be delayed three days at Syracuse—though he become wind-bound at Rhegium—though he tarry seven days at Puteoli with the brethren, aye, and though he suffer persecution and martyrdom at Rome—will land at last in glory through the grace of God. "For so an entrance shall be ministered unto you abundantly into the everlasting kingdom of our Lord and Saviour Jesus Christ."

> "Oh spread thy covering wings around
> Till all our wanderings cease;
> And at our Father's loved abode
> Our souls arrive in peace."

So may it be with each voyager. Amen.

Other Related Titles

THE GOSPEL FOR THE PEOPLE by Charles H. Spurgeon
Sixty Short Sermons, with a 34 page Sketch of Mr. Spurgeon's Life, and Fourteen Portraits and Engravings, with a Preface by Pastor Thomas Spurgeon. These Short Sermons were selected by Thomas Spurgeon (his son) from the Series with a view to their being used in Mission Halls, and other similar places. They are about half the length of the ordinary Sermons.

THE EVERLASTING GOSPEL by Charles H. Spurgeon
Only a few days before Sir Robert Phayre received his Lord's summons, "Come up higher," he had completed the selection of Sermons here published, and given instructions for them to be bound in a volume for his own use. He had also chosen the title as printed on the present title-page, and the passage of Scripture (1 Peter 1:18-25) which he wished to have inserted there as a kind of motto for the whole series of discourses. The gallant general was a regular reader and an ardent admirer of Mr. Spurgeon's Sermons, and in his opinion the thirty-six here collected formed by themselves a most timely testimony against many of the prominent and pernicious errors and heresies of the present day.

COMMENTING & COMMENTARIES by Charles H. Spurgeon
A Reference Guide to Buying the Best Books
"This is a guide for buying and using Bible commentaries of many kinds, made entertaining by the pungent good humor of the author, Charles Haddon Spurgeon. It is an invaluable resource for ministers and theological students, as well as all Bible students, introducing them to the riches of the best of what has been written about the Bible in past generations."- Joel Beeke

FROM THE PULPIT TO THE PALM BRANCH
A Memorial to Charles H. Spurgeon
This impressive volume is a true celebration of the life of "The Prince of Preachers" with special focus on the last months of his life, his death and the twelve remarkable days which followed. This rare volume contains the very last addresses delivered by Spurgeon in the last month of his life.
"Many will be happy to know this long-unobtainable volume on Spurgeon is to be available again. I have collected such books for years but not yet owned this rare book. May the recovery of Spurgeon's memory lead many to the devotion to Christ which so marked his life!" - Rev. Iain H. Murray

www.ingramcontent.com/pod-product-compliance
Lightning Source LLC
Chambersburg PA
CBHW071138090426
42736CB00012B/2148